AN ECONOMIC *QUERIST*

AN ECONOMIC
QUERIST

G. L. S. SHACKLE

CAMBRIDGE
AT THE UNIVERSITY PRESS
1973

Published by the Syndics of the Cambridge University Press
Bentley House, 200 Euston Road, London NW1 2DB
American Branch: 32 East 57th Street, New York, N.Y.10022

© Cambridge University Press 1973

Library of Congress Catalogue Card Number: 72–96679

ISBN: 0 521 20188 8

Printed in Great Britain
at the University Printing House, Cambridge
(Brooke Crutchley, University Printer)

CONTENTS

This book is dedicated to
Mark Perlman

PREFACE

When, in seeking to understand some face of Nature or the human world, we arrive at some *direct question* (a question with a question-mark), which we have succeeded in putting into words, we have already in some degree broken into the closed mystery of things. We are already in some sense looking in through a gate, we have some glimpse of the character and arrangement of things inside. It follows that one effective step, which can be taken by anyone who wishes to convey to others some insight which he may suppose himself to have, is to suggest to them such a question and propose his answer to it. This is the method adopted in this book. The act of formulating an efficient question is itself part of the struggle to make sense of things. That act is the first which the investigator, the explorer of any field, must perform. Thus the questions and the answers in this book stand on the same footing. The questions it proposes are such as renew themselves in my mind every time I consider afresh some part of the field which has been (rather arbitrarily) demarcated during the three latest centuries as 'political economy'. It is hardly needful to say that I do not claim these questions to be the best (let alone the only!) ones that can be put. But I wish to be thought of as putting them to myself. If the reader cares to listen in to the debate, he may perhaps find himself in some sympathy with me in the endeavour to give a seeming orderliness to the seething phenomena of business. The answers which I here offer to my own questions are, of course, in large part the results of the thought of others. But many of the questions are, I think, somewhat different from those which are implied by the orthodox text-book treatment. And a number of the questions are of an import which could by no means be contained in the standard accepted outlook of economic theory. That established theory rests on the premiss that men choose their conduct in the light of fully-informed reason. The assumption that human beings ever are or can be 'fully informed' on every matter and circumstance which can affect the sequel to any specified available act of theirs is, so far as I can see, absurd and easily shown to be so, unless we opt for a determinist view of the Scheme of Things. Such determinism, the view that history is a book whose pages are being merely turned, not written, as the moments pass, makes the notion of *choice* an empty one, a mere clicking of the machine as it works. But economics is *about* 'choice'. These views, which regard determinism and therefore 'full information' as importing insoluble dilemmas into our thought, but which for many or most economic theorists are heterodox and even heretical, have been given their freedom in these pages.

The title which I have given this book draws its inspiration, of course, from that of Bishop Berkeley's work *The Querist*. Except for knowing that this work contains some '500 questions' in the broad field of human economic and political affairs, especially as illustrated in the Ireland of his day, I must not be supposed to claim much acquaintance with it.

I hope that the index of this book will be of much greater service to the reader than the ordinary index of a work of theory. He will find in my index, I hope, a ready means of tracking down each of the principal ideas which this book offers. Those phrases which I judge to have the status of technical terms, with a fairly exact specialized meaning, I have put in italic in the index. This book was written between 6 November 1971 and the early spring of 1972.

G. L. S. SHACKLE

8 March 1973

I wish to record my gratitude to Mrs E. C. Harris for her invaluable help in seeing this book through the press.

G.L.S.S.

I

EXCHANGE

What is exchange?

Does it take two people to make an exchange? Not when one
and the same person has before him a choice of this or that. If
he takes *this*, he will in effect be giving *that* in exchange for it.
He will be giving up one thing, in order to have another.
Exchange is choice, and choice is the act of a particular person.
What he chooses may be such that he needs another person's
agreement, another person's choice. But we can look at the
action of exchange through the eyes of one person at a time. It
involves preference and sacrifice. It is deliberate. It gives
advantage.

How much advantage does exchange give? Are not things
which can be exchanged for each other by publicly offering one
of them for sale in a market, and publicly buying the other for
the same price in the market, equal in price? Are they not then
exchanged without gain or loss? But does it follow that price
measures preference? Gain will be in terms of preference, for a
person is only a gainer if he thinks himself a gainer. These
questions can all be disentangled and made to yield a coherent
scheme of ideas.

How can I measure the strength of a person's wish to have a
particular thing, an ounce of tea or of butter? By seeing how
much of something else he will exchange for it. This is the only
way. And if this is the only *operation for measuring* the strength of
the wish, this also is the only *meaning* of 'the strength of the
wish'. The length or the mass of, say, a brick remains virtually
constant in all ordinary circumstances. But the strength of the
wish for an ounce of tea does not remain constant. It varies
with circumstance. The measurement we get by seeing how

much of something else he will give up varies according to whose wish we measure, what other kind of thing is to be exchanged, what other things he is already provided with and how well or badly provided, and in especial, how well or badly he is *already* provided with tea.

What does *provided with* mean? If I have an ounce of tea, I am provided with tea, for today or this week, but not for this month or year. *Supply* cannot be measured just in ounces or litres. It needs also a reference to an interval of time. 'Four ounces per week' is a supply. Five ounces per week is more desirable, the object of a stronger wish, than four ounces. But how much stronger is this wish? What *extra* quantity of butter would a person give up in order to have five ounces of tea, instead of four? Would he offer the same extra quantity of butter, in exchange for one extra ounce of tea, no matter whether the *extra one ounce* of tea was the difference between four ounces per week and five ounces, or the difference between sixteen ounces per week and seventeen?

When he is very comfortably off for tea, with an assured supply of sixteen ounces a week, what difference to his comfort does an extra ounce make? Though it is the *same* extra quantity of tea, will it be worth the sacrifice of as much extra butter as if the supply of tea were meagre? The strength of the wish for a larger supply seems to depend on the size of the existing supply.

What is a market?

How does a person choose one course of action out of many which suggest themselves? To choose a particular course is to reject all the others. How can we classify the elements of his situation, which push him towards one course rather than another? He has *interests*, purposes which he desires to achieve. Their character is influenced or settled by his tastes, his qualities of mind inborn or born of experience and education. How far can he attain his desires? This depends upon his circumstances. Every element of his situation, which we do not classify as part of his tastes, we classify as part of his circumstances. Within that latter comprehensive class, what kinds of thing are included?

First, his endowments. These comprise his capacities of brain and hands, and his material possessions. Secondly, the whole scheme of things, both in the general sense of what the world is and how it works, and in the more particular sense of the immediate state of that world. Under this second heading there is a sub-class of special interest. It consists of the intended actions of other people. For as in a game of cricket, the result of a batsman's stroke depends on the actions of the fielders, so in life at large my actions, your actions, have their sequel shaped by what other people do. Choice of conduct, then, seems to arise from the confrontation of a man's tastes and his circumstances. But this leaves out a vital matter. He cannot adapt his conduct to make best use of his circumstances, unless he knows what those circumstances are. How can he know?

And in especial, how can he know what actions of other people will occur at the same time as his own action is eliciting its consequences, its sequel? For some at least of those actions of others are being chosen now, at the moment when he is choosing his own action. And since the 'he' and 'him' of whom we speak is the general member of society, anybody and everybody, how can we suppose that *everybody* knows what the others are choosing before he makes his own choice? It is this enigma that is solved, for a particular kind of action, by the market. The market solves the paradox of simultaneous inter-dependent choices, when those choices are concerned with *exchange*.

General pre-reconciliation of actions. General equilibrium

The answer to my problem, what action of mine will best serve my interests, best satisfy my desires (and those desires may be selfish or unselfish) depends upon the answer to questions such as: What is your action going to be? The answer to my problem will be a, b or c, according as your action is going to be x, y or z. I can write down a list of different actions (for example, different quantities of my farm-crop that I would put on the market), one for each of your possible actions (for example, different prices per bushel you would offer for my crop). If each member of a society (a village or a nation) makes such a list of conditional actions, and all these lists are collected and compared, it may be possible to find out one action for each person, such that this would be his preferred action provided that each other person performed some stated action similarly prescribed for him. This *pre-reconciliation of conditional intentions* solves the paradox of rational inter-dependent choice, the problem how each person can choose his action in the light of *reason fully informed*, the information having to include the choices made by others at the same time as his. Such pre-reconciliation is what the market, in a rough practical way, achieves. When the market works perfectly and brings the totals of all quantities offered and demanded into balance in this way, the result is called a *General Equilibrium*.

How does the market pre-reconcile choices?

When the actions to be chosen are those of exchanging some quantities of some goods for some quantities of others, the chooser does not need to know the itemized lists of conditional intentions of all other people, but only the total effect of these offers. How much can I get of this good and that, in exchange for this or that quantity of the good which I can offer? is what he needs to know. These rates of exchange, or prices, are summaries of the effect of the pre-dispositions of the people composing the market. Thus the market has three duties. It must gather information, distil it into knowledge, and deliver that knowledge to every person in the market. These three duties are all done at one stroke, by means of one notion, that of *price* expressed in terms of a single good. Each good on the market is assigned a price in terms of one and the same good for all of them. In a perfect market, each good has only one such price at any one moment, and a person will not be able to get more beer for his butter by exchanging it first into cloth and then the cloth into beer. If he could get a better price by round-about

4

exchanges, this would mean that pre-reconciliation, the assignment to every person of his best action, given a similar best for everyone else, would not have been carried through.

How does the market discover the right prices?

A price is not right, if it induces more offers to buy than to sell, or the opposite. For in such a case, there will be *unsatisfied* choosers of action. Some people will be led to choose actions which are not available to them. 'Wrong' prices mean that the market has failed in its duty of gathering information and distilling it into knowledge. If a price is 'too low' it will seem attractive to 'too many' would-be buyers. They will try to buy more than sellers are offering. There will be a gap between the higher price they would pay for this too-small offered quantity, and the price at which it is apparently offered. Some of them will march into this gap, offering somewhat higher prices than the ostensible market price. The market price itself is thus raised. And this raised price will induce some larger offers to sell than heretofore. The price will be 'right' when it equalizes the total quantity offered of the good, and the total quantity demanded. For then it will be allotting to each person such actions, and only such actions, as he can in fact take.

Is there bound to be a solution?

The notion of an equilibrium is the notion of a solution, a solution to the problem: Can individuals choose rationally their inter-active conduct? By rationally we mean here 'In such a way that each can rigorously demonstrate his chosen course of conduct to be the one, of all those available, that goes furthest in achieving his aims.' 'Those available' will be a list constrained (limited) by the condition that every member of the society, the market, has equal freedom and equal relevant knowledge of his own circumstances. In speaking of *inter-active* conduct we remind ourselves that every person's choice of his own conduct contributes to shaping the circumstances of every

5

other person's choice of conduct. Is there, then, bound to be an equilibrium? It is plain that in the most general setting of this question the answer must be no. Obstacles from many sources could, in general, block the existence (the logical possibility) of a solution. But we can list those restrictive assumptions, those limitations of generalness, that will give the best chance of the existence of a solution.

One of these conditions is the operation of the principle: The larger your supply of a good, the less acute (in given circumstances) will be your need to increase it. 'Acuteness of need', 'strength of desire' we have decided to measure by the quantity of one good that would be surrendered in exchange for a *given extra* quantity of another. The quantity of A which must be surrendered for an extra unit of B is the market price of B in terms of A. The quantity of A which a person is *willing* to surrender for an extra unit of B need not be the same as the market price. Suppose it is greater? Then he will be the gainer by making the exchange. When he has thus increased his supply of B by one unit, his need for a further extra unit of B will, by our supposition, be less acute. In the course of further such exchanges, the stage will be reached when the quantity of A which he is *willing* to give up, and the quantity of A which it is *necessary* to give up, to get an extra unit of B, are *equal*. That is the point for him to stop the process, the process of increasing his supply of B by reducing his supply of A.

When he, and every other member of the society, or the market, has thus considered every good in his list and effected an all-round adjustment, the General Equilibrium will have been achieved. It will have been achieved for exchanges of goods on one particular occasion. But life does not consist of one particular occasion, we look forward to others. And this is the greatest of all obstacles to a meaningful General Equilibrium.

If we confine ourselves to 'one occasion', we are not involved with the question whether supply is a stock, so-and-so many barrels, tons, *et cetera*, or a flow, so-and-so many barrels *per day* or tons *per year*. But if we insist that supply is a flow, this is because we look forward. We have a practical conscience, which compels us to think of dates which are still remote. Or we have a restless imagination, which recognizes its freedom to fill the future. But if such deferred dates are real to us, so also must be the notion of choices which will be made at those dates. And deferred choices cannot be pre-reconciled, the notion of *anticipating a choice* is a contradiction in terms. It follows that, in the ultimate analysis, strict rationality is not compatible with thoughts of tomorrow.

When all members of the market have so adjusted amongst themselves the quantities per week of the goods that each gets from other people, and the quantities per week of other goods that he gives in exchange to other people, that the ratios of exchange which he is willing to adopt for *small extra* quantities given up or received are the same as those which the market prescribes, then it follows that all members of the market have become *unanimous* in accepting these market prices as the right ones. Public (that is, market) prices thus seem to be not merely personal judgements made by individuals but also objective facts external to their thoughts, facts as unarguable as the weather. And thus it might seem that market prices make possible those calculations which the economist is constantly engaging in, the measuring of the size, in some useful sense, of vast, inexpressibly various collections of things, the things which make up the year's general 'national product', or the amount of goods-in-general which society uses up in a year, and so on. For if everything has a publicly agreed and established market price, the values of all the different kinds of thing, according to their price and quantity, can be worked out and added up. And does not price express and measure desirability, usefulness?

Does market price, then, express usefulness, the very kind of thing that the economist is interested in? In claiming to do so, it practises two illusions in which two truths are neglected. One truth is that market price expresses the desirability of a little *extra* supply of something, and not the desirability of the entire supply, as a whole, which an individual is receiving. If I have enough air to breathe, a little extra air is of no consequence.

If I do not have enough air to breathe, some air is worth all I possess. The second truth is, that the ostensible unanimity of the market concerns the relative values of goods to each person individually, not their relative value, in a basic sense, to *different* persons. The comparison of values between persons is not a thing which can be done publicly, 'objectively'. It can be done only by the individual conscience of each person for himself. If he has such a conscience, he will vote for laws which put right, in some degree, the obvious harshness of life for some by taking a little away from others.

2

INTER-NECESSITY

What good is exchange?

If it benefits *A* to give butter and get beer, how can it benefit *B* to give beer and get butter? It can do so if *A* has too much butter in proportion to his beer, and *B* has too much beer in proportion to his butter. What is the right proportion of beer to butter, for *A*? It is that proportion which leaves him indifferent between those *small extra* quantities, which can be had in exchange for each other. How does *A* come to have the wrong quantities, in relation to each other, of butter and beer, and *B* also the wrong quantities, though quite different ones? It may be that *A* is a dairy-farmer and *B* a brewer. They belong to a system which provides for the desires of all its members by *specialized activities*.

The activities which compose such a system are *inter-necessary*. Each sustains, and is sustained by, the system as a whole. They are like the organs and activities which compose a living creature: breathing, heart-beat, digestion and so on. It was the likeness of economic society to a living organism which struck François Quesnay, the royal physician at the Court of King Louis XV, and inspired his *Tableau Economique*. The Economic Picture showed a society composed of Farmers, Landowners and Artisans. The Landowners provided the Farmers with fields and the Farmers tilled them. A part of the crop was seed-corn, the rest was divided between sustaining the Farmers, paying rent to the Landowners, and buying manufactures for the Farmers from the Artisans. The Artisans received their share of the crop, not only direct from the Farmers, but partly also from the Landowners, who ate a part of their share and passed the rest on to the Artisans in exchange for manufactures. The share received by the Artisans was used by them partly as food and partly as raw materials of their manufactures. Thus the system maintained itself, and each of its three sectors, perpetually in being; the flow of goods into and out of each sector being technologically appropriate to maintain each other without deficit or surplus. This technological balance was symbolized in Quesnay's *Tableau* by assigning equal values to the inward and outward total flow of each sector taken by itself.

Quesnay's *Tableau* in itself constrains, but does not determine, the size of the flows of goods between its sectors. The flows into and the flows out of any sector must be able to support each other technologically. But this condition would be satisfied by a great range of different sets of flows. How can the *Tableau* be made self-sufficient as an account of economic society, able to answer all questions which can be put to it in its own terms? The *Tableau* is a picture of an unchanging society. It does not pretend to answer the question: How has this unchangingness come about? What preserves the unchangingness? If we insist on asking those questions, we must provide some such answer as: The people do not look further ahead than to the next harvest, they are content with their settled arrangements and feel no wish to change them. The society which Quesnay described is in a sense a momentary society, one where past and future are meaningless. In this hand-to-mouth, year-to-year society, effectively timeless as we saw the General Equilibrium to be, the conception of General Equilibrium is elaborated into a society where *exchange* is not merely exchange of goods between persons, but also exchange of means for ends, exchange of the powers of fields, farmers and their tools for food and manufactures. It includes *production*. Thus the *Tableau* helps to enrich the representation of an economic society offered by General Equilibrium. In return, General Equilibrium offers a possibility that the system of inter-necessary activities described by the *Tableau* may be shown to be in suitable conditions *determinate*, that is, having flows of goods of a size which reflects the tastes and endowments of the individuals composing its sectors.

The *Tableau Economique* has a modern version. The purpose

of the *Tableau* was anatomical, to give the King of France a conception of how the organs of economic society fit together. It did not ask nor explain how the scale of one sector came to stand in such-and-such a relation to that of another, nor what might change these relations, nor what principle would govern the effect upon them of a given shift in those tastes which underlie the uses people make of their endowments. These questions about proportions and their changes were considered by Wassily Leontief in his input-output analysis.

What is an industry?

It is a collection of such firms, industrial plants, and processes of cultivation, extraction and fabrication, as we care to put together on the ground of some affinity amongst their products. Not all industries that are likely to be thus defined will sell their products only to the ultimate enjoyers of those products. Many or most of them will pass on their product mainly to other industries for further processing. Farms send grain to the mill and the mill sends flour to the baker, wells and mines send petroleum or ore to be turned into chemicals, rubber or metal to make trucks which serve every other industry. But the fringe of this vast network of conceptual 'goods-ways' along which products of many industries converge upon each single industry and the product of that industry is distributed to many industries, consists of retailers who sell to consumers or the government, the *final users* of the end-products of the productive organism as a whole. When these final users change the proportions in which they demand this kind of good and that kind, a complex wave of changes of demand spreads inwards from the retailing fringe through the whole interior of the net, and even if only one or two kinds of final product are affected, every intermediate product, every product sold by one industry to others, will feel an increase or decrease of demand sooner or later and in some degree. In what degree? It is a general and comprehensive answer to that question that Leontief's analytical scheme is designed to provide.

In a cooking recipe, the proportions of the ingredients are fixed, but the absolute amounts are not fixed. The cake can contain one egg and two ounces of butter, or two eggs and four ounces of butter, and so on. In the Leontief scheme, the first stage is to write down the recipe of each industry's product in terms of the quantities of the products of other industries required per unit of this industry's product. In order to make meaningful addition possible, the quantities throughout are given in terms of value at fixed prices. The value of product i required per unit of product j is called an *input co-efficient*. When this input co-efficient is multiplied by the annual quantity to be produced of product j, the answer is the annual quantity required of product i for the purpose of making j. Now j can be the label of any industry. When we have thus run through the whole list of j's, the whole list of industries, and added together the answers, we have the total quantity of product i required for intermediate use, that is, for use in helping to produce other products. The list of industries will include industry i itself, which doubtless uses some of its own product. (For example, a paper-mill may keep its accounts on some of its own paper, a coal-mine may drive its hoists by burning some of its own coal.) At the end of the list of quantities of product i annually required for intermediate use, the quantity of i annually required for *final use* is written down. Now we have accounted for the whole of the annual quantity required of product i. The same procedure can be used for every industry (i is a label which can be attached to each industry in turn, just as j can be). In the end we have, for *each* of the n industries, an equation showing how the total annual quantity of this industry's product is used up. There will of course be n such equations, and they can be written down one below another so that the input co-efficients, considered by themselves, form a square of n rows and n columns. It was this kind of pattern which, long before any application to economics was thought of, suggested the branch of mathematics called matrix algebra, which nowadays (aided by the computer) is the means of turning our system of equations 'inside out' to yield desired information.

What can be done with our system of equations?

The system of equations we have obtained contains the cooking recipes of all industries. It contains them in a certain form, namely, it shows for *each* industry, i, the manner in which its total annual quantity of product is absorbed by, and is dependent on, the total annual quantities produced of all products, and the final-use quantity annually required of product i itself. But what we really want, for Leontief's purpose, is this information in a different form, namely, the total annual requirement of product i in terms of the final-use quantities of all the industries' products. To obtain the information in this second form, from the system of equations giving it in the first form, is to *solve* the system of equations. The technical procedure need not concern us here. Its result is to give us the recipes of the products in a shape where we can see the effect, on the *total* annual quantities required, of any given change in the *final-use* quantities required.

Why is it useful to have the information provided by input-output analysis?

If shifts of final demand from one product to another can be conjectured, or are envisaged by government policy, the effects of any such shift can be prepared for, by directing investment into one kind of industrial facilities rather than another.

Is the idea of inter-necessity, illustrated by Quesnay's Tableau *or by Leontief, a central one in economics?*

Without it, the economic affairs of society would make little sense, and the formulation of policies for national societies and for the world would be done in the dark and could have only parochial aims which disregarded the universal interest.

3

PRODUCTION

What is production?

Production is making something. To make something you need materials. Things which help to make something are themselves thereby more or less changed. Some of them entirely lose their initial form and appearance, and 'go up in smoke'. Others have their substance incorporated in the thing which is being made. Their shape and perhaps their texture even so are usually altered. Some things which help to make others are not visibly changed at all. They are tools in the ordinary sense. At the end of helping to make something they are a little blunter, a little looser in their joints, and need repair. Thus production starts with one collection of things, and ends with another. Production is an activity of changing the form of things, not conjuring something out of nothing. And yet something is conjured, else what would be the sense of taking so much trouble? What is produced by production?

Production is not, in its essence, making things, but *making things useful*. Production is putting things in shape to serve our needs. Production is made up of changing the location of things (by mining and transportation), changing their constitution (by smelting, forging *et cetera*) or shape (by rolling, extruding, cutting) or chemical nature (by reaction with each other) or their internal organization (by assembly, or by encouraging a life-process).

What is the test of success in production? It lies in making possible survival and enjoyment. The desire to go on living from this moment to the next is part of what it is to be a living creature. For humans this is not enough. They imagine, and desire to achieve, beauty, insight, authority or saintliness. All these ambitions require in some degree the adaptation of their surroundings, the bending of circumstance. The bending of circumstance to men's desires is production.

Can there be a general *theory of production?*

Production takes a million different forms. The materials, the tools, the skills, the end result, differ from case to case. Is not *productive knowledge* the kind of knowledge possessed by the miner concerning mines, the farmer concerning flocks and fields, the engineer concerning stresses and strengths, the printer concerning type, the weaver concerning cloth? Is not productive knowledge the knowledge of crafts and technologies? How can there be a theory of production in general, short of an encyclopaedic catalogue of every method known to industry? It is surely true, and little recognized by economists, that the business man is deeply immersed and vitally involved in problems of technology. In these days the rivalry of businesses is increasingly the rivalry of technological inventors, seekers of novelty in products and productive methods. If there were a general theory of production, it would properly consist of the general principles of manipulating material, if such principles can be discerned. The 'theory of production', so named by economists, is not, in its main bearing, about making the product but about sharing its market worth amongst those who have contributed their efforts and the services of their possessions to making it. It was the problem of explaining why this and that group of contributors to the making of the general produce as a whole receive this and that proportion of the whole, that was suddenly found to be capable of solution by studying a particular aspect of production.

*The general produce consists of
a myriad different kinds of objects and services.
How can we think of it as
'a single whole', capable of being divided up
in determinable shares?*

Quantities measurable on a single scale, as lengths and weights are, can be called *scalar*. Economics gains much of its appeal to the policy-maker and the administrator by offering a means of 'scalarizing' assemblages of diverse things. It can do so because it can assign to each of them a measure which appears to be publicly agreed and therefore objective like length and weight. This measure is the market value of an object. When all the items have been given a value by the market, these values can be added together. When the list of items includes everything which has been produced by the society in a week or a year, each item being so-and-so many physical units each priced at so-and-so many money units, all these values can be added up to yield a total value of weekly or annual production. This total is the society's aggregate income.

What determines incomes?

The theory of the division of the society's total annual produce, its total income, is rather confusingly known in the literature of economics as the problem of distribution. In the eighteenth century, this problem concerned the division of the income amongst groups of people who were deemed to perform fixed economic duties. These classes were thought of as, for example, landowners, labourers and the owners of stocks (inventories or outfits) of materials and tools, and they were said to receive respectively rent, wages and 'profits of stock'. No solution or explanation of the question why the result of the collaboration of these components of society should in practice be divided amongst them in such-and-such proportions was found, until the whole problem of the relative prices of things was given a unified and inclusive answer in the *marginal analysis* which was established in the thirty years after 1871.

What is a marginal *quantity?*

A marginal quantity is a *difference* between two measurements which have something in common in their circumstances. They may be measurements made at different times of one and the same object, or type of object, which, despite some continuing identity, shows progressive change in some respect. Such a difference need not have been actually measured, it may be merely the yet-unknown answer to a question. A person may consider two possible sizes of his supply of tea, four ounces a week and five ounces, and he may ask himself how much he would pay for the extra ounce. Here we have *two* marginal quantities placed beside each other. Marginal quantities are only interesting and illuminating when two of them, bound up with each other by their natures or the circumstances of their measurement, are compared.

What makes such comparisons interesting or useful?

An extra ounce of tea per week will involve some particular extra weekly expenditure. The extra ounce will, perhaps, be deemed by the potential purchaser to matter less to him, and to be worth fewer pence, when it is extra to a large weekly supply than when it is extra to a small one. To get the most comfort, enjoyment, satisfaction, out of a given weekly budget (planned or affordable expenditure) a person should evidently arrange his shopping list so that the transfer of a shilling from tea to butter (or vice versa) would give him no over-all improvement in his comfort. If we like we can say that the marginal (the extra) satisfaction from a marginal shilling (an extra shilling) of expenditure should be the same no matter what it was spent on. Such an example may seem trivial. But in other contexts, ostensibly on a larger scale, the insight the 'equi-marginal principle' can give may seem more impressive.

How does marginal comparison apply to production?

How much is it worth a business man's while to pay in weekly wage in order to have an extra worker? As much as the difference such an extra man will make to the value of the business man's weekly production. Let us remember what is the measure of production. It is value *added*. In reckoning production, we allow for the materials used up, the wearing and deterioration of the tools. Production is value created over and above this using-up and wear-and-tear. On a farm with its particular fields, in a factory with its particular buildings, plant and machines, an extra man can be extra to a small or to a large existing force of workers. If this force of workers is small in relation to the fields to be tilled and the flocks to be tended, or to the tools and facilities to be kept in operation, an extra man will be acutely needed and highly valuable. If the work force is very large in relation to this frame of other resources, he may find little which is useful to do. 'An extra man' has a different significance, will make a different difference, according to the quantities of various kinds of productive means with which he is to be combined. There is some reason and evidence to believe in a *law of diminishing marginal productivity* for means of production, having somewhat the same form as the law of diminishing marginal satisfaction of the consumer of products. The need and usefulness of an 'extra layer' on the heap of units of some commodity, or of some means of production, will be more, or less, insistent according as the pile is only small or already large, in relation to the quantities at hand of other things which form the background of its enjoyment or employment. Such relations between the quantity employed of this or that factor (means) of production, and the weekly or annual amount of production resulting from the collaboration of all factors, can be succinctly expressed and combined in a *production-function*.

What is a production-function?

It is to be expected that a change in the quantities of men, machines and natural resources employed in making something should affect the weekly or yearly quantity produced of that thing. Can such effects be reduced to rules of calculation, or a general formula enabling us to work out what change in output will result from such-and-such a change in the quantity of some means of production? Such a formula would be a production-function.

A quantity is surely a single and unique number of units. How can it make sense to speak of a *variable* quantity? When a set of measurements have something in common in their circumstances or in the nature or identity of the measured object, they can be considered together, and a different member of the set can engage our attention on different occasions. The variability consists in the freedom to shift our attention from one member to another of the set of measurements. Each individual member of the set is called a *value* of the variable. The measurements composing a variable can have been actually made, or they can be merely conceived. A dairy-farmer planning his enterprise can pass in review various possible acreages for the pasture-land he will acquire, and various possible sizes of the herd he will put upon it. According to these two quantities of means of production (other circumstances being given) his weekly supply of milk will be larger or smaller.

What can we do with the notion of values of variables?

We can take one value from each variable in some list of variables (one measurement obtained, actually or imaginably, from each item of a list of measurable things) and treat this set of values as composing a unified object, a thing-in-itself. That object will be a *vector* or *point*. What is a point on the map? It is something defined by reference to lines of latitude and longitude. Latitude and longitude are numbers. So a point on the map is a *pair of numbers*. A point or vector is a set of numbers considered as one thing, and capable of being represented, when there are only two numbers, by a single thing, namely a dot within a frame of reference-lines. Every place on the map is such a point. But not every place on the map of the North Atlantic lies, let us say, on the Great Circle from New York to Bantry Bay. We can set up a rule or test for admitting some points to a 'club' and rejecting all others. If such a rule or test works by stating some relation to be fulfilled between the numbers (the values) composing any point which is to be accepted into the 'club' the rule is a function. The formula $s \equiv \frac{1}{2}gt^2$ says that only those points (s, t) will be admitted which have, for any freely-chosen t, an s obtainable by multiplying t by itself and by half g. If s is thought of as some number of centimetres, t as some number of seconds, and g as the 'acceleration due to gravity', 981, then the formula gives the respective distances through which an object would fall, if unimpeded by the atmosphere, in various numbers of seconds after it was released.

Must we have a formula if we wish to express a function?

No. Since any one point can be represented (when it is a 'two-number' point) by a dot within a frame of reference-lines, a class of points selected by a function-rule can be represented by a class of dots. If the function-rule is a simple one, like $s \equiv \frac{1}{2}gt^2$, the result of marking in a series of the dots selected by the rule will show a corresponding simplicity of arrangement, a visible architecture. This particular formula will be pictured as a parabola or fountain-jet shape. Even a diagram like this is unnecessary. The pairing of values, one value from each of two variables, can be indicated (for a sample of such pairs), by simply writing the paired numbers side by side in two columns. If there is in principle an infinity of such pairs which the function selects, we can of course thus represent only a few of them.

What does a function express?

It seeks to express some part or aspect of the architecture of the Scheme of Things. If we divide the Scheme of Things into non-human Nature on one hand, and human affairs on the other, we are likely to try to find functions describing human affairs. This will be easier where Nature and human doings overlap, as in technology, for Nature seems to have a steadiness which restless ambitions deny to humanity. Technology is the exploitation of natural principles for human purposes. The principles are the same, whether exploited or merely observed, and by carefully preserving some set of background circumstances unchanged, we can find functions to represent the measurable design of the natural universe. Dairy-farming is a technology, and the number of weekly gallons of milk may be expressible as a function of the number of cows, the number of acres of pasture, and other details of the dairy-farmer's outfit.

What is the use of a production-function?

For the economist, it is the idea itself of a production-function which is illuminating. At the outset, we might be willing to suppose that such a function could have any one of very many conceivable characters. But there is reason to claim that one such character is especially natural and central. If, without making any other changes, the dairy-farmer doubles his chosen number of cows, and at the same time doubles his chosen number of acres of pasture, will he not thereby double his expected weekly supply of milk? A production-function of such a character that a doubling, trebling, *et cetera*, of every one of its quantities of means of production will also respectively double or treble the weekly or yearly quantity of product, is said to show *constant returns to scale*. Such a character is plausible, provided our list of means of production is inclusive enough. For if we had two identical dairy-farms, side by side, each would produce the same output of milk. Then by simply declaring that these two farms are to be considered as one farm, we have a doubling of all the measurements. If now it is also true that when the dairy-farmer, planning his enterprise, makes step-by-step increases in the supposed quantity of some one means or *factor* of production, while leaving the others unchanged, he finds that equal steps of the increasing factor yield diminishing steps of output, then the production-function idea gives the economist an answer to one of his most central problems.

How is the produce of collaborative resources divided up amongst those who provide them?

The early economists spoke of wages, rent and the profits of stock. They took one of these at a time and sought an explanation of the size of the aggregate of this kind of income. Wages, they thought, were subject to the 'iron law' that any incipient improvement of the standard of living of wage-earners would be destroyed by the increase of their numbers which it would induce. Rent they accounted for by the parsimony of Nature in furnishing only so much of the best soil, which compelled the price of corn to rise till it could cover the cost of cultivation of poor soil, at which level it afforded a surplus or rent to good soil. And so on. But there is a great question looming. When each kind of income has been explained and its size in principle determined, will all of these kinds of income, at the sizes thus arrived at, together amount to just the total which is available to be shared and has to be accounted for? Unless this sum comes out right, we have not explained the dividing-up of the society's income, the aggregate income which measures its total production of a year. For unless it comes out right, we shall have explained away more income than there is, or else we shall have income left over whose disposal we have not accounted for. This is the famous *adding-up problem*.

What solves the adding-up problem?

It cannot be solved so long as we invoke a distinct principle for each distinct kind of contributory productive service. A guarantee that all the factor-bills, the results of multiplying the number of employed units of each factor by its pay per unit, will add up to the value of the product, can arise only from some single, general principle which applies to all factors no matter what special names or features we assign to them. We have found such a general principle in the idea that each factor will tend to get that pay per unit which is equal to the extra value-added due to an extra employed unit of the factor. But this unity of principle for the pricing of factors of production carries us only part of the way. We need next to invoke the claim that a production-function's natural and inevitable form, given that the factors of production can each be divided up as finely as we like, is that which gives constant returns to scale. Combining the two ideas of diminishing marginal productivity of each factor when increased by itself while the others remain the same in quantity, and constant marginal productivity of a general equi-proportional increase of all factors together, we get the kind of production-function that is subject to *Euler's theorem*. Euler was not an economist but a great mathematician. Yet for more reasons than one, economists should honour him as one of the greatest members of their profession. For he enabled them to complete and close the theory of value and distribution and demonstrate its self-contained perfection, a perfect self-sufficiency, granted the conditions which it stipulates.

What does Euler's theorem say?

It says that in a function like the production-function we have just described, the number which is the numerical value of the function is equal to the sum of the marginal quantities each multiplied by the numerical value of its own variable. This rigmarole is far simpler than it sounds. The word value as we use it here means *numerical value*, a particular number belonging to that set of numbers which constitutes some variable. One of our variables will be the number of men employed by the farm or the firm. Multiply it by the extra value-added which the farm or firm would secure by a week's work of one extra man. Another variable will be the number of acres of pasture. Multiply it by the extra weekly value-added due to one extra acre. And so on through the list of variables. Then add together the results of these multiplications of particular numbers of workers, acres, *et cetera*, by the marginal products of that given number of workers, acres, *et cetera*. The answer, if the production-function is of the right character, will be equal to the number of weekly units of product.

Euler's theorem is a mathematical truth which in its essence and own nature has nothing to do with economics. It is, so to speak, a sheer piece of luck for the economists. Or we can claim it as a proof that human affairs are as basically orderly as those of Nature in a narrower sense. On either view, Euler's theorem sets a seal on value theory, by enabling it to show itself as self-contained and complete.

4

PRICES

What do prices do?

We saw prices as knowledge necessary to an equilibrium. They are the solution of a problem, namely, how many units of this good must exchange for one unit of that good, throughout the list of all goods, in order to reconcile amongst all individuals the conditional intentions which result from their particular desires and endowments. In practice, the solution is not found at one stroke, and for a sole and timeless occasion of exchange, by collating statements of how much each person would give of this or that good in exchange for what quantities of other goods, but instead it is approximated by the market in a continuing response to streams of such offers.

How does the market respond?

It is the solution or equilibrium as a whole which determines (settles) each price. If a single price were different, every price would in principle be different. Thus the essentially truthful picture of the market's manner of responding to a shift in the tastes or in the endowments of some of its members, is to suppose the entire system of co-valid equations, which expresses the conditional offers of each member throughout the list of all members, to be solved afresh after the affected equations have been appropriately re-formed. But this ineffably complex picture is beyond the mind's power to grasp in detail. Insight is to be had only by blotting out the greater part of such a picture, in order to get a close-up of some small, intelligible part. To do this is to adopt the method called *particular equilibrium*. Particular equilibrium analysis relinquishes accuracy and completeness in the interest of simplicity. It says: Suppose all (money) prices, except that of one particular good, were to remain fixed, how would the weekly quantity offered, or asked for, of this good respond to changes of its price? To suppose all prices fixed except one is in strictness a contradiction of the idea of general inter-dependence of prices. Yet it allows us to consider the *types* of adjustment, in the quantities and ratios of exchange of each good for each other good, which make up the picture as a whole. When, in a throng of people, one person lurches against another, the movements of these two can be considered without proceeding at once to remind ourselves that the whole throng will sway and re-act in some degree to the initial disturbance.

How can conditional intentions be expressed by an equation?

An equation consists of four kinds of symbols. In order to give ourselves the greatest freedom in assigning meaning to the equation, those of the symbols which stand for numbers are initially written as letters of the alphabet. Such a letter is like a pencil point, which can rest first on one and then on another of the items in a list. The list of items here in question is a list of numbers, each of which is to be looked on as a member of a class of measurements, actual or conceivable. Measurements form a class of this kind when they have something in common in the objects or the circumstances of the act of measuring. Such a class of measurements can be called a variable quantity. A particular number which is a member of that class is called a value of the variable.

Some of the letters in an equation stand for variables in the above sense. Each such letter can have assigned to it any numerical value (any number) belonging to the class of numbers which constitute that variable. Other letters stand for single, unchanging numbers. They are called constants. They serve to give this or that degree of 'leverage' to the variables. The throttle of a motor-cycle engine can be open to various degrees, and the engine will accordingly propel the machine at more or less speed, but the bore and stroke of the engine, and its gear ratios, will remain the same, and these constant design features will determine the precise effect of opening the throttle to this or that extent. Evidently when we look at a different type of motor-cycle we may find a different set of 'constant' design features. Besides the symbols representing variable or constant numbers, there are symbols which instruct us to do something, such as to add, subtract, multiply or divide. Lastly, there is the 'equals' sign which asserts that the pattern of symbols standing on its left comes to the same number, when the instructions it contains are carried out, as that on its right.

Now suppose that in the terms composing the right-hand side of the equation there appears only one variable, even if the letter representing it is present in several terms, and that this variable is the price per unit of some good. And suppose that the left-hand side of the equation consists of one letter only, representing the list of possible quantities that might be bought each week by some individual. This solitary left-hand letter is a variable. It represents a list of possible quantities, only one of which, however, can in any particular case be the true one. Various quantities 'might be bought'. But which particular quantity will be bought? The answer depends on what the price is. If, instead of the letter representing all possible prices, we insert a particular number as the particular price which we suppose to prevail on some occasion, and do the calculations indicated by the right-hand side of the equation, the answer will be the number of physical units (grams, litres, *et cetera*) bought weekly by the individual concerned. His intention to buy a named quantity is conditional on the price being such-and-such. If we write z for the number of litres which will be bought, and x for the number of pence per litre, the equation might read:

$$z = 20 - \tfrac{1}{2}x.$$

At a zero price, 20 litres will be bought, at a price of 2 pence, 19 litres; at 4 pence, 18 litres; at 20 pence, 10 litres, *et cetera*.

The equation expresses the *condition* on which any named action within this context depends.

Why is there a minus sign in the right-hand side of this equation?

It has the effect of making the quantity bought (according to the equation) smaller when the price is higher.

What are the grounds for supposing that a lower quantity demanded will correspond to a higher price?

The grounds need to be very carefully set out. They illustrate the meaning, and the difficulties, of particular equilibrium. 'A boat which is loaded will be in more danger of running aground than one which is in ballast.' Is this true for any and every comparison of no matter what boats, in what seas, regardless of the state of the tide in the respective cases? Can we select any two boats at random, no matter when we see each of them, no matter where or what they respectively are, and say that the more heavily loaded one will be nearer to running aground? Of course not. No one would dream of such an assertion. It is no less dangerous to treat the quantity demanded of any good as depending solely on price and as always declining when price rises. In order to treat weekly quantity demanded as depending solely on price, we have to assume that all other circumstances than price are either irrelevant or unchanging in face of the change of price. This supposition is shortly referred to as *ceteris paribus*, 'other things equal'.

When a person's supply of something is small, he will devote this small daily or weekly quantity to those uses where his need for it is most acute. When there is very little water, it will be drunk, not used for washing. To satisfy the most acute needs, it will be worth while to pay a high price, that is to say, to go without other very desirable things. If a person is to feel it worth while to satisfy less acute needs for the thing in question, the sacrifice involved in getting the extra quantities for these further needs will have to be a less serious sacrifice, the giving up of smaller quantities of other things, a *lower price*. To satisfy his less acute as well as his most acute needs for the thing in question, a person will have to buy a larger weekly quantity of it. Thus a larger weekly (*et cetera*) quantity bought will be associated with a lower price. This lower price will be one and the same for all the units bought. This will be true not only for each individual considered alone, it will be true for all individuals taken together. If, for each conceivable price of the particular good whose particular market we are studying, we add together the quantities that would respectively be bought by individuals at that price, we shall get two lists whose items are paired with each other, one item from each list. This will be a demand-schedule showing what weekly quantity of the good in question will be bought in the market at each of the conceivable prices. As we glance down the list of prices from high prices to low, the corresponding quantities will go from small to large.

What are the 'other things' that must be supposed unchanging?

The incomes of the people concerned; the prices of other goods (especially those goods which serve nearly the same purpose (substitutes) and those which are needed in conjunction with the good in question (complementary goods); these are the circumstances directly relevant. Substitutes, or competing goods, need not be technologically similar to the good whose purpose they can serve. Communication can be by paper and ink or by telephone; entertainment and education can be by books or by television. Goods are complements to each other when both are needed together in order to achieve some end, as paper and ink or pencil, cars and petrol and tyres. The cheapening of a substitute will weaken the demand (desire at each given price) for the good we are considering, and, other things equal, will lower its price. The cheapening of a complementary good will strengthen the demand for our good and tend to raise its price. Because of these potential effects, particular equilibrium requires us to suppose that no change of price of substitutes or complements of the good we are studying takes place.

*In the equation of demand, a larger quantity demanded
is associated with a lower price.
But what if people in general come to have
a more pressing need or stronger taste
for the good in question?
What change of price will reflect their desire
for a larger quantity?*

An equation of demand, written with particular constants such as the 20 and the $\frac{1}{2}$ in our example: $Z = 20 - \frac{1}{2}x$: expresses a *given* state of mind, or state of need, of the individual. If that state of mind, his degree of liking for the good or his appreciation of its usefulness or indispensability to him, *change*, then we shall have to re-write the equation with different constants. For example, we might find that his new attitude to the good is represented by $Z = 30 - \frac{1}{3}x$. This would mean that at *any* particular price from $x = 90$ to $x = 0$, he would decide to buy a larger quantity than before.

*Are there, then, two quite distinct ideas to bear in mind
about the way a variety of prices is associated
with a variety of weekly quantities demanded?*

The distinction we have very carefully to make is between the association of large quantities with low prices, and small quantities with high prices, in a *given* state of people's tastes, and the association of any named quantity with a higher price per unit than was offered for that quantity before, when there has been a *change* in people's tastes, a strengthening of their desire.

How does supply *respond to price?*

If the market price of some product rises, what can then be done that could not be done before? When the firm asks itself 'Will it pay us to increase our weekly quantity of product by one barrel, or one ton?' the answer at the old price will perhaps be 'No. The extra expense of production which the extra barrel (*et cetera*) would involve us in, would be more than the extra sale-proceeds that the extra barrel would give us.' But at the higher price per barrel or per ton, it may be that the extra expense of production, due to an extra weekly unit of product, would be covered. Then the question presents itself to us: If, at the old price, the 'topmost' unit of output (weekly quantity produced) was covered by the addition it made to sale proceeds, why should not the extra cost attributable to an extra barrel be similarly covered? An obvious *possible* reason is that an extra barrel makes a larger addition to the total expense of production, the larger the weekly number of barrels already being produced. Why should this be so?

What is marginal *cost?*

Marginal cost is the *difference* between the total cost of producing N weekly barrels or tons, and the total cost of producing $(N + 1)$ weekly barrels or tons. In deciding how much to produce, a firm may be supposed to pass in review a number of different possible sizes of output. Beyond some size of contemplated output, it may find that each extra unit on the pile of contemplated output makes a bigger difference to the total cost of producing all the weekly units, than the one below it. This circumstance must be due to an increasing difficulty or resistance which the piling-on of extra units of output encounters. What can such difficulties be? They can fall under two heads. The difficulties can consist either in *obtaining* extra units of means of production or in *fitting them in* to the existing productive outfit.

What is the difficulty of fitting extra units in?

It arises if the quantities employed of only some, but not all, of the means of production can be increased. For when some of these quantities are increased, but the others left unchanged, this alters the proportions of some means of production to each other. If, at the going rates of pay for people and for acres of land, the existing proportion of people to acres is right, a different proportion would be wrong, from the viewpoint of the employing firm. If extra workers, but not extra acres, can be obtained, this may be the only way of increasing output. But it will mean that each employed worker will be less well supplied with land than before. His pay will be too high for his reduced efficiency, *unless the price of the product is increased.* When we asked what can be done when the market price of the product rises, the answer is that the output can then be increased *despite difficulties.*

What is the difficulty of obtaining extra units of means of production?

What were these extra units doing before the firm in question sought them? If they were unemployed, they may be glad to join the firm for the same pay as is already being earned in it by similar units. And there will be no one discouraging them from doing so. But if they are already in employment elsewhere, some increase of pay may have to be offered to induce them to come to our firm. And their present employers may resist this move, by offering increased pay themselves. Extra units may each cost more than our firm has hitherto paid for each of the ones it is already employing.

How can the effect of these difficulties be expressed?

What is that effect? It is the implication that if an increase of output of some product is to be quickly elicited, a higher price per unit will have to be forthcoming for it. On the supply side, in contrast to the demand side, a larger weekly quantity may be associated with a higher price per unit. This will have to appear in the *equation of supply*. It might, for example, look like this:

$$S = 8 + \tfrac{1}{4}x.$$

Here S is the number of physical units weekly produced, and x is the price per unit. The term containing x has a plus sign, meaning that as x is assigned larger and larger numerical values, S will have also to be assigned larger and larger numerical values. In the equation of supply, when it expresses the immediate effects of an endeavour to increase output quickly beyond some level, output and price typically increase together.

How do the equation of demand and the equation of supply fit together?

Let us make these equations refer to a whole market, rather than to an individual demander and an individual supplier. If the market is to be claimed to work successfully, what test will it have to pass? It will have to ensure that all demands are supplied, and that all supplies offered are demanded. But are these two conditions compatible? What can bring them into conformity with each other? The circumstance which they have in common is the price per unit. Can a price be found which will satisfy both equations at once?

How can the test of market success be expressed?

It will be expressed if we write $S = Z$, namely, weekly quantity supplied equals weekly quantity demanded. But since we have an alternative expression for Z, and another for S, the equality of S and Z implies the mutual equality of these alternative expressions:

If $\qquad Z = 20 - \tfrac{1}{2}x, \quad S = 8 + \tfrac{1}{4}x \quad \text{and} \quad S = Z$

we have $20 - \frac{1}{2}x = 8 + \frac{1}{4}x,$

$$12 = \tfrac{3}{4}x,$$

$$x = 16.$$

A price of $x = 16$ makes the quantity demanded

$$Z = 20 - \tfrac{1}{2} \times 16$$

$$= 12$$

and makes the quantity supplied

$$S = 8 + \tfrac{1}{4} \times 16$$

$$= 12.$$

A price of 16 money units per unit of the product will 'clear the market'.

When the taste for a good becomes stronger, what happens to the prices of its means of production?

Services and materials which are together capable of producing a good are the technological equivalent of that good. If the good comes to command a higher price, these means also will be worth more than before. They will be worth more to the industry which produces this good. If, because of this, the means of production flow abundantly into the industry and enable it to produce a larger supply, the price of the good may not rise as far as it would otherwise have done. Whether, in the end, it will have risen at all will depend on the general re-adjustment which, if the change of tastes had time to work out its effects before other changes supervened, would reflect the change of taste. That change may comprise not only a stronger desire for one good, but a weaker desire for others. If so, the industries making those other goods will be willing to release means of production, which are now worth less to them. Prices steer resources to those industries where, because of the demand for the products of these industries, the resources can earn most. But, if we suppose time to be given for full re-adjustment of everything to everything else, no means of production, no type of skill or tool, will be able to earn more in one industry than in another. It will be able to earn a wage, or a rate of hire, equal to its marginal value-added to the output of any industry where it finds itself. Prices are the means of *allocating* resources to the activities where they do best for the society at large, provided the incomes of its members are 'equitable'.

What, then, do prices do?

They serve as the steering-gear of the economic society, the gear by which the society steers its own ship. The steering-gear of a ship does not decide where the ship shall go. It merely gives effect to the decisions of the captain. And his decisions themselves are not free of constraints. He can go only where the water is deep enough, and where his fuel is sufficient to take him. Tastes and needs; endowments, including human capacities, natural resources and man-made facilities; natural laws so far as we know and can use them; these are the elements which shape each person's economic conduct and the combination of all those individual actions to compose the general course of society's affairs. The implications of these combined elements are expressed as prices, which signal to individuals their appropriate actions, selecting from the conditional intentions of each person that realizable intention which best suits the conditions.

Prices, confronted with his tastes, inform a person what is his best attainable mix of satisfactions. Confronted with technologies, they inform the firm what are its best methods of production. Confronted with the capacities and tastes of a potential producer, they inform him what is his most advantageous job. The performance of each of these duties by the price-system depends on its performance of all of them. Every price is involved in all prices and all prices are involved in every price.

Such is the ideal picture. Reality does not match it. But the insight which it gives is far better than nothing.

What measures the leverage of price-changes in effecting quantity changes?

The measure is called *elasticity*. If a one percent reduction of price effects a two percent increase of quantity bought, the *price-elasticity of demand* is two. If a three percent increase of price effects a one percent increase of weekly quantity supplied, the price elasticity of supply is one-third. The total *revenue* of a firm is its sale-proceeds of product, namely, number of units sold per time-unit multiplied by price per unit. If the price-elasticity of demand is numerically greater than ONE, a reduction of price will increase revenue. If the elasticity is equal to ONE, any small price-change will leave revenue virtually unchanged. *Net revenue* is revenue less expense of production. Will net revenue be increased by a change of price? This depends on the answers to *two* questions: how much will the resulting increase of weekly quantity produced and sold increase the total expense of production, and how much will it increase the total revenue? The best output will be the one up to which extra slices of output have each added more to revenue than to expense, but beyond which the *next* extra slice of output will add more to expense than to revenue. The test of best level of output is: marginal revenue equals marginal cost.

5

TIME

What is a chapter headed time *doing in a book on economics?*
The themes which our questions have so far centred on compose
a theory where time apparently has only one obligation, to keep
out of sight. In the Theory of Value which arose in the second
Victorian generation, time is present only in the most impover-
ished form. In so far as it gives time any role at all, that theory
is not self-consistent. For the faith which inspires that theory is
that men can, and do, choose their conduct *rationally*. They
choose it (in the Theory of Value) so as to get the utmost
satisfaction of their desires, and realization of their ambitions,
which their circumstances can be made to yield. Conduct is
rational when it can demonstrate success in this endeavour. But
to be able to *demonstrate* that he has exploited his circumstances
in the most effective way, a man must know, perfectly and for
certain, what his circumstances are. A proof, concerning the
use of circumstances, evidently requires to be able to refer to
circumstances relevantly fully stated. We have already seen a
difficulty, that amongst each man's circumstances are the contemporaneous choices of other men. But there is a far worse
difficulty. It is not only their contemporaneous choices, but the
choices they may have the opportunity to make in future, which
are relevant. And we can be far more general in our statement
than this. Our lives are lived *on the edge of the known world*. For
only that world is known, which has already *emerged into the past*.
Time in its conventional guises, in the masks which astronomers,
dramatists, historians compel it to wear, is the mere analogy of
a space, a dimension. We think of time as an 'extensive
variable'. In the history books, all dates are co-valid. All points
of time exist *together* in the historian's mind. But in the mind

37

of the person living his life of actuality, no two moments ever co-exist. There is only the present. All thoughts are thought in the present, whether they are thoughts about classical antiquity or the twenty-second century. And it is surely, in strictness, misleading to speak of thinking 'about' the twenty-second century, when one is living in the twentieth. For the twenty-second century is not there to think about. Anything we think concerning it, we have to invent, to imagine. There is a large freedom to do so, the freedom of the void of future time. How can a man know all about his circumstances, when the vital part of them does not yet exist? For the conduct which we are free to choose is *future* conduct, but the circumstances which we are able to know are *past* circumstances. That is why the Theory of Value in its strict form, the theory of rational conduct, must place itself in a timeless world, a world of a single moment which has neither past nor future.

What formal scheme can embrace things recorded after they have happened, that is, ex post, *and things imagined as able to happen, things conceived* ex ante?

The science of the movement of inanimate bodies does not concern itself with a double question: What has happened? What is going to happen? but rather with a single question: What is happening? Which view is the more fundamental? It might be argued, I think, that the physicist's way of speaking telescopes two ideas. There is first what he can observe, namely, what has already taken place no matter how recently. Secondly, there is his inference, from his knowledge of the effect of forces or of their absence, that what is about to take place will be a regular continuation of what has taken place, like it in essentials even if it includes acceleration or higher derivatives. The physicist does not envisage change of laws, change in the way things work, change in the way the world's phenomena are fundamentally related to each other. As to change in the forces which are operating, he can exclude this by supposition, or by controlled experiment. Thus what *has* happened and what is *going to* happen can be seen as a unity. And for a long time, and even today, economists have unthinkingly assumed that these methods of thought were appropriate to their own concerns. In this they overlooked a vital difference. For inanimate bodies are not influenced in their behaviour by conscious knowledge of their own, nor by the lack of such knowledge and by the character of substitutes for it which they may invent. By contrast, what individuals, thinking humans, do springs from their thoughts, and those thoughts are not regular continuations and outgrowths of their immediate past but are subject to sudden mutations, even originations, as new suggestions are noted and interpreted by the individual in the course of deciding his actions. Human conduct, and the course of affairs which results from the inter-action of the conduct of different individuals, requires the more fundamental view, the recognition of a difference of nature between what we can say, at any moment, about the past and what we can say about the future. The physicist, by a sophisticated procedure (the procedure of considering an infinite series of shorter and shorter time-intervals such that we can always find one which is greater than zero but shorter than any pre-assigned non-zero length) is enabled to speak of velocity 'at a point' of space or of time. For the economist, this will not do. For him, the relevant object of study is an interval in which effect is given to thoughts existing, in his own mind and the minds of others, at the threshold of this interval; effect whose character depends on the character of those thoughts, but does not by any means necessarily conform to any one individual's thought. Such an interval, thus conceived, cannot be telescoped until it vanishes in a point of time. It must have a beginning and an end, separate and distinct from each other, and such that the view of the content of the interval which can be imagined at its beginning is part of the source, but is not the image, of the view which will have become visible at the end.

*Yet, is not the notion of decisions taken by everybody,
independently but simultaneously, at discrete moments
separated by an interval for the working out of their
consequences, a highly unreal construction?*

It is, and the only answer to such an objection is to ask what
better method can we find? People, of course, are impelled by
circumstance to take decisions; problems which they have never
considered, and could not earlier have formulated, are suddenly
presented for their solution. They do not wait for some prescribed date to arrive before making up their minds. A steady
rain of individual decisions pours down to form the stream of
history. Yet Myrdal's invention, encapsulated in the phrase *ex
ante–ex post*, thrusts upon us an absolutely vital point: decision
refers to the future and prescribes action to be taken in a time
whose circumstances, determining the outcome of that action, we
cannot know; when we are able to know the circumstances and
the consequences of this decision and action, those consequences
will have happened and will belong to the past. Business,
and life at large, is a scurrying throng of events and confused
disorderly inter-actions, not the orderly sweep to-and-fro of a
Greek chorus or of the dancers in a minuet. But the essential
fact of our human predicament, that we are obliged to act without knowledge, to act first, know afterwards, must somehow be
built into our theorizing. Myrdal put his finger upon a vital fact
to which the idea of equilibrium had made economists blind.

*Having recognized that decisions made by individuals,
without some special means of pre-reconciliation
such as a market, will be based on
inconsistent suppositions and will often lead to
disappointment, what can we go on
to infer about the next round of decisions,
made in the light of the disconcerting outcomes?*

Almost nothing, if we hope to base such inferences on sweeping
and self-recommending assumptions such as the one which

underlies value theory, that men act rationally in their own interest. A person's reaction to the failure of his guesswork can, for all we know, be anything within wide bounds, if any bounds at all can be discerned. He may drive on in the belief that his chosen course was right but not powerfully enough backed up; or he may retreat and adopt a quite contrasting course. The set of self-recommending axioms on which a purely deductive economics could be raised was a narrow base for sweeping laws and could apply only to a highly artificial world, the timeless world of perfectible knowledge. When we abandon the assumption that the participants in business and in history at large have, or can conceivably have, anything remotely approaching perfect knowledge, we thereby deny to *ourselves*, as detached observers, any possibility of perfect knowledge of what people will do.

But are there no plausible suggestions to be made about how business men will react to a given kind of failure of their expectations?

Yes, there is the highly credible notion of the *cumulative process*. If prices offered for their products, or the quantities demanded at given prices, turn out to be higher than the business men had counted on, will they not be tempted to make preparations for larger outputs for the future? Those preparations will consist in arranging for larger supplies to themselves of the products of other firms, in making improvements and enlargements of their own durable equipment, in engaging extra labour. In seeking to do these things, they will themselves have to offer somewhat higher prices, and pay out larger incomes to their suppliers and their employees. When those increased incomes come to be spent, they will further re-inforce the unexpectedly strong demand which gave rise to them. The self-re-inforcing process of increasing outputs and prices will be in being.

How far, and how long, will it go on?

This question opens a theme which, in the earlier decades of this century, was in the forefront of discussion: the nature and mechanism of the old nine-year cycle of boom and depression in business, which came to be regarded as an established fact of observation. Answers were proposed in great number and variety. One such depends on an eventual self-defeat of expectations through their building too boldly on their own initial effects. The growth of general output and of employment and of aggregate income may lead, it is suggested, to a firm belief that this growth will persist indefinitely. The flow of enterprise-investment may rise swiftly to a scale which counts upon that growth, and having risen to that high level, will level off rather than rise further. But it is the *rise* of enterprise-investment which was the source of the rise of incomes. When enterprise-investment ceases to rise, income will cease to rise, and this cessation will betray the expectations which led to the rise. Thus the whole house of cards will tumble down.

If the nine-year business cycle has been in abeyance for thirty years, can it have vanished forever?

The dramatic, complete and totally unforeseen transformation of the business scene and climate between the 1930s and the quarter-century following the Second World War has discredited any reliance on mechanical models or analogies and permanently stable mathematical functions as means of interpreting history and preparing for its transformations. In the early 1970s in Britain we have at one and the same time a pace of general price-rise which halves the value of money in a decade or less, and unemployment threatening to approach that of the early 1930s. It is time for economists to concern themselves with the thoughts that create conduct and not treat that conduct as the operation of a machine.

6

MONEY

What is the use of money?

Prices are ratios in which goods exchange for each other. Can a good have more than one price in terms of some one other good? Not if all the ratios of exchange are mutually consistent. If one ounce of tea can be exchanged for two ounces of butter, and one ounce of butter for four ounces of sugar, and six ounces of sugar for one ounce of tea, the price of tea in terms of sugar is eight ounces, or six ounces, according to the sequence of exchanges. But if the market is performing perfectly its duty of diffusing to all its members a knowledge of every offer to buy or sell anything, there can be no such inconsistencies, since they would mean that some persons were making exchanges at ratios less favourable to themselves than other ratios which were available. In a perfect market, every good will have only one price in terms of any one other good. And in order to do sums conveniently, it will be necessary to have one good agreed upon as the one in terms of which all prices shall be expressed. Such a good is then serving as a *unit of account*, and this is one of the duties performed by money.

Agreement upon one specified good to serve as a unit of account is a *convention*. With this convention there may well go another, that the good which is a unit of account shall always be accepted, at the market rate of exchange, whenever it is offered in exchange for something that someone is willing to sell at the market price. If so, the good which serves as a unit of account is also serving as a medium of exchange. However, this second use, unlike the first, presents us with a puzzle. Why accept, in exchange for the good one is offering, anything except that particular other good which one desires at the

moment for its own sake, for the sake of its physical and technological properties? Why go through two operations of
exchange instead of one? This question is not asked in the text-
books. We are so used to selling a thing for money, and then
buying something else with the money, that the question why
we do not directly buy the second thing with the first, at a
market price conveniently expressed in the unit of account, does
not present itself. But we must ask and answer it. The answer
is a momentous one. It is that at the moment when we sell something (a week's work, or a season's crop) we do not necessarily,
or usually, know what we want to buy. The question that the
value-theorists did not ask, except as a tiresome after-thought,
is how the necessary knowledge, of many matters and of many
kinds, is gained by the person who has to make choices of conduct. Of course, direct exchanges of goods wanted for their own
technological sakes, as food, fuel, clothing or means of transport,
would require a central organization where accounts could be
kept and values set off against one another. But it would not
require any *storing* of a *medium of exchange*, any holding of a
reserve of purchasing power. In fact the role of money as a
medium of exchange is in these days quite trivial. It would not
be convenient to write a cheque for a bus fare. The record of the
value we have used up by using the bus, out of the common
pool of production, is most cheaply kept by handing over coins
or notes. Buying and selling for large values is done by means
of ledger entries. And a centralized ledger account for everyone,
which had at all times a balance of zero, is perfectly conceivable,
if only people were always able to decide, at the instant of
receiving value, just what physical form that value should be
embodied in. The *use of chequing accounts*, and the *keeping of a
store or reserve of money*, are two entirely distinct ideas, separable
in meaning and even in practice. The need for money as a
store of value is an aspect of the basic, irremediable and permanent insufficiency of knowledge, and this insufficiency of knowledge is an aspect of time itself, which washes away knowledge
(the relevance and applicability of knowledge) as the tide
carries off the daily flotsam of the sea. When today's needs have

44

become yesterday's, we must make up our minds afresh, for tomorrow and many tomorrows which are too distant yet for any decision about them. Money, when we keep it in stock, is what enables us to put off deciding what to buy.

Why put off deciding what to buy?

If a thing is desirable, do we not desire to have it *now*? If profitable and able to yield us an income, is it not better to have that income as soon as possible, so that it may quickly accumulate and yield us more income? Why keep money, whose obvious use is to be got rid of in exchange for something else? Should we not expect people to do just that, to get rid of money by exchanging it, as soon as it comes into their hands? There is a mystery here, since people do not part at once with all the money they receive, but keep a store of it.

We are not asking why they do not *consume the equivalent* of every pound they receive, the moment they receive it. The answer to that is easily seen. Wages are paid weekly and salaries monthly. To eat and drink the whole week's wages on Saturday would leave us to starve. But why pile up more and more money, more than enough to go to the end of the week or month? If we have a stock of money that need not be spent on consumables, why not spend it on tools, houses, shares in business firms? These things may be counted on to yield services or income. Money itself, when instantly available, may not. One answer is that we may not be able to feel sure precisely what we shall need. It would be very awkward to have to make out a shopping list for a whole month ahead (with no possibility of changing or supplementing it) even if we could store all the goods involved. But there is another reason. The price of things, in terms of money, may change.

The prices of things that are wanted for themselves, goods 'in the flesh', seem nowadays always to go up, but the prices of businesses as going concerns, the prices of shares in such businesses, do not by any means always go up. Neither do the prices of acknowledgements of debt. The prices of income-earning assets can go down as well as up. Why buy them at a price higher than they will stand at next week, or next year? *But who knows?*

It is not stupid (it may prove unlucky, or it may prove lucky) to keep a stock of money which could buy us income-yielding assets, if we suspect that the prices of those assets are about to go down. If we felt sure they were about to go down, it would be natural to sell the ones we already have, to exchange them for money. If everyone thought such prices were about to go down, and everyone acted on this belief by selling their assets, or trying to sell them, the prices would indeed go down with a vengeance, and go on going down until some people changed their minds, and began to think the next price movement would be up. Stable prices for long-lasting assets can happen only when there are two opposite opinions in the market. For if there is only one opinion, the prices of such assets will move in the way this opinion supposes.

The market for long-lasting things is necessarily, in some degree, a speculative market, it is a market where people buy things, not in order to use them, but in the hope of selling them again later at a profit. No one can buy unless there is someone willing to sell, and a person willing to sell is one who believes in a coming fall of price. He prefers to have his wealth in the form of money itself.

What are the forms of wealth?

The forms of wealth, of long-lasting things with a market value, are of course as many as we care to distinguish. But it is useful at any rate to divide them into three large categories. There are in the first place all kinds of useful *equipment*. This class comprises all material objects and systems which help us to stay enjoyably alive. It includes the drained and tilled fields, the standing forests, the wells and pits, the flocks and herds, the houses and all other buildings, the transport systems, industrial plant and every kind of tool. Underlying such equipment there is the frame of nature herself. But for the immediate purpose we shall include Natural Resources in the category of equipment. Secondly, there is money, whose nature we are enquiring into. And thirdly there are a borrower's promises to make payments in future in return for money handed to him now. (His payments will comprise both re-payment of this money, and a compensation to the lender for disadvantages which are inseparable from lending.) Equipment nowadays composes vast systems whose ownership is divided into tens or hundreds of thousands of shares. For our present discussion we need not distinguish those shares from the equipment they represent. The first and third of our categories, the non-money assets, are bought and sold on markets in exchange for money, they have money prices which are influenced by every kind of circumstance which can give rise to a thought in a man's mind. It follows that the question in a man's mind, shall I keep my stock of money or shall I exchange it for equipment or for promises to pay, will depend for its answer largely on how he thinks the money prices of those assets are going to move in the immediate future. They are speculative assets and the markets for them are speculative markets. Such markets are quite different in vital respects from the markets where consumers buy the means of sustaining life.

What like is a speculative market?

A speculative market is one where the buyers and sellers look to future dates. If a person is to conceive something to be going to have a price at a future date, that thing must promise to last, in some sense, until that date, or to be going to be engendered at that date from things already existing, like a crop from the seed already sown. Speculative markets deal in *effectively durable* goods. They deal also largely in things which are more suitably conceived as a *stock* rather than a *flow*. And most of all, they are governed by influences quite different from those tastes of consumers and those expenses of production which govern the flows of consumer goods. The taste among people generally for butter, the expense of keeping cows, are the governing circumstances which press upon the price of butter. But an existing stock of something does not have to be produced, except that it has to be stored. And the demand for it is not a demand to consume but a demand to keep for future sale, a speculative demand. And a speculative demand is not a rational, therefore not an analysable, demand. For reason can work only if there are data to apply it to, and if those data are relevantly complete. Whence are the data to be found, concerning every rumour, every accident, every novel invention, every political or diplomatic or social upheaval, every eddy in History's tide, which can seem to be able to bear at some deferred and remote date on the price of a stock of goods which may be offered for sale at that date?

Speculative markets are inherently restless. A speculative gain can be made only if there is a price-change. Price-changes must therefore be welcomed, encouraged, deliberately conjured out of nothing. Speculative markets are eager for straws in the wind, omens, rumours, claims to Second Sight. When the prices of non-money assets are subject to the obscure manipulations and the incalculable tides of reasonless opinion which a speculative market engenders, money can often seem a very consoling form in which to hold wealth. There is a *speculative motive* for holding money, as important as the motive of being ready to make payments when the occasion for them has arrived or crystallized. Both the speculative motive and this other one, called the transactions motive, take their origin in the irremediable, basic absence of knowledge of an unwitnessable future. Money is a refuge from uncertainty.

In the round, then, what is money? Money is what money does. It fills several needs. Its logically first nature and task is that of a unit of account. Market prices are expressed in terms of it. It could serve this purpose without having an existence any more material than that of the 'runs' scored at cricket. But accounts can be kept by other means than marks on paper or magnetic traces in a tape. They can be kept by handing tokens about, just as the cricket umpire starts the over with six coppers in one hand and calls the end of the over when he has transferred them all to the other hand. These tokens are given in nominal, notional, account-keeping exchange for goods wanted for their own sake. They are stand-ins for some other real goods which will eventually be acquired as the counterpart of what is now being sold. They are a medium of exchange. As a unit of account, money need have no other existence than in the mere momentary act of registering an exchange of equal values, one basket of goods for another, both counting (at the prices of that moment's market) as the same number of money units. If the system of exchange and accounting is so organized that nothing takes place except simultaneous exchanges of goods for goods of equal value, then money balances will always be zero and no *stock* of money will exist at all. But such a system would lose us one of the great advantages of money, a service rendered by it which goes right down to the roots of conscious existence and joins economics to the Nature of Things. For if money is allowed to exist as a stock, it can enable a seller to put off deciding what to buy. And in the complicated life of today, the freedom to do this is pressingly, indispensably needed. When money exists as a stock it is serving as an *asset*, an embodiment of wealth. In this guise finally it serves, or imposes itself, as a speculative counter, a 'medium of gambling'. For gambling is an inherent, unavoidable part of any economic society which uses long-lasting assets and buys and sells them on a market.

How does money come into being?

The money which comes into being, in the sense intended by our question, is the money which can serve as an asset and as a reserve of purchasing power. And that money will only possess general purchasing power, the ability to buy anything at any time from any potential seller, if it is believed by every individual seller to be acceptable to every other potential seller to whom he may wish to pass it on. 'Acceptability' is a wholly conventional quality, something conferred by the tacit spontaneous agreement of everyone concerned. A particular type of garment is fashionable if everyone wishes to be seen wearing it, and everyone wishes to be seen wearing it if everyone else is seen wearing it. Acceptability in general exchange is the prime requisite of anything which is to serve as money. It will also conveniently and naturally be denominated in the unit of account. Thus an established 'money' is the unit of account on which some elusive but genuine existence has been conferred by writing a number on a piece of paper, or in a ledger, and solemnly declaring 'This number stands for so-and-so many units of account.'

Who has the right and the power to create money by writing on paper a number declared to stand for units of account?

A bank has this power. A bank can put the name of its customer at the head of a page of its ledger, and write there that it owes this customer £100. Where did this £100 come from? It is the counterpart of another page of the ledger, where the customer's name is written as owing the bank £100. By the act of writing this mutual indebtedness, the bank has given its customer the power to make payments. The customer's cheque, drawing on the £100 which the bank has created for him, will be accepted by tradesmen in settlement of his debts to them. But in the background of this process, must there not stand some central and authoritative source of 'official' money? If we are to speak of one pound sterling, must there not be a Bank of England to write *that* piece of paper? A central bank writing official money, an authority stamping official coins, are a usual and convenient part of the machinery. But they make no essential difference. What does the Chief Cashier of the Bank of England mean when he says, on his banknotes 'I promise to pay one pound'? He means no more, nor less, than 'I declare this piece of paper to be money.' And the Bank of England could, in a conceivable system, be the only bank. The creating of money is the act of writing a number on a sheet of paper, and declaring that this number represents so many of the units of account; provided this is done by someone who has the general consent of society for his action.

Then, can anyone be a bank?

When a moneylender lends money, he hands to his customer the pieces of paper written by the Bank of England. But suppose instead, he handed out an IOU signed by himself, and suppose further that the borrower found he could pay his own debts with this IOU. Then the moneylender would have become a bank, for he would have succeeded in putting money of his own creation into public circulation. It may still be objected that his IOU refers to money written by the Bank of England. Then let us go a step further. Suppose the moneylender, Mr Blank, writes a piece of paper saying 'This is 10 units of Blank's money', and gets this accepted by his borrower because the borrower finds that he, in turn, can get it accepted by other people. Mr Blank would then have successfully usurped the privilege and power of the Bank of England. It is inconceivable, in fact, that he could do so. But this creation of money by simple fiat, by uttering, as the grammarians say, a performative sentence, is just what the Bank of England does.

Money, ultimately, is created by consent. This consent is exercised through some formal machinery which includes a means of regulating the number of units of account which shall circulate in the society. In Britain this regulation still relies on a law of the land by which those to whom money is owed need not accept anything except the notes of the Bank of England in discharge of their claims. Thus any other bank, a 'commercial' bank, which creates money by writing simultaneously in its ledger a debt of its customer to itself and a debt of its own of equal amount to its customer, is restrained from pushing this process too far by its obligation to give Bank of England notes on demand in discharge of any debt of its own to a customer. And the number of Bank of England notes which will be available to it and the other commercial banks, all taken together, for this purpose is regulated by the central authority, that is, by the Treasury and by Parliament itself.

If money is so different from goods useful in themselves, *what are the influences bearing on the prices of goods in* terms of money?

The 'theory of value and distribution' undertakes to explain how, in a highly abstract and artificial situation, the prices (exchange ratios) of goods in terms of each other would be settled. That theory, despite the abstraction of the setting in which it could be rigorously defended, can fairly be supposed to operate in the real world also, though in a manner disturbed, confused and obscured by many powerful forces, and by the great gulf or total unlikeness which exists between its assumptions and the real Scheme of Things. But that theory has seemed in past times to say little about the way in which *money* labels are attached to real goods. And in the early 1970s the nature of money has revealed a new, alarming and uncomprehended aspect, which seems to render existing theories, if not obsolete, at least irrelevant.

What theories about money *prices have there been?*

There have been two main kinds of theory. One kind is mechanical or, we can better say, *hydraulic,* and assumes that money moves around in identifiable packets and can only be accused of affecting prices at some place and occasion if it is present there. Moreover, in this hydraulic view, the speed of its movements is constrained by society's business habits (such as the habit of paying wages weekly, salaries monthly, rents quarterly, and of only taking cash to the bank at intervals of a week or a day instead of 'all the time'). Money, in this conception, only affects the price of a good when it is in process of being exchanged for that good. In the theory of value, the central, essential and characteristic act is *exchange*, and it is the exchange of ephemeral, perishable goods like the fish and eggs of a primitive society. In such exchanges, the respective quantities actually changing hands are the visible and (in the philosopher's language) the 'efficient' causes or governing circumstances which make the price to be so-and-so. Even in these exchanges, the quantities exchanged merely reflect deeper and more 'original' sources, namely, the desires and thoughts of the exchangers. But when the things to be bought and sold are durable, and will have prices at future dates as well as prices now, the matter is obviously far different from what prevails in a market for farm eggs and fresh milk. The question what those future prices will be is the one whose answer would tell us whether a given price paid now would prove profitable or the reverse. Who knows the answer? Nobody knows or can know it. Yet 'the news' floods in with endless suggestions for surmise, guesswork and gambling. The markets for durable assets, whether these are tangible individual objects like houses or ships or machines, or whether they are shares in companies owning these things, or whether they are a borrower's promise to pay stated sums at stated dates, are, by the essential nature of the things they deal in, *speculative* markets, existing only in virtue of humanity's inherent ignorance of what will crystallize from the void of time. And the prices which thus arise in one of those markets, the market for borrowers' IOUs, the bond-market which covers, in our subject's jargon, all British government securities and similar promises, are from a different viewpoint the *interest-rates* which new borrowers in effect must pay and new lenders can obtain. The second theory of how money prices are pushed up or down involves these interest-rates, to whose meaning and determination we must turn.

7

DISCOUNTING

What is an interest-rate?

Lending is the exchange of money in hand now for a promise
by the borrower to make payments of stated amounts at stated
dates deferred from now. A lender, who hands over such a sum
of spot cash in exchange for such a promise (a bond) cannot
feel sure, when he does so, that he will not wish, at some
unknown future date, that he had his money back; some urgent
need of it or some golden opportunity for using it may arise.
What will he be able to do in such a case? The bond promises
payments at stated dates, not 'on demand'. If the lender's need
for cash should happen to arise before the borrower's payments
are due to have restored a sufficient sum, there is only one thing
the lender will be able to do. He can seek, in that case, to sell
the bond to a third party, who will thus become the lender. At
what price will he be able to sell the bond? There is no knowing.
His act of lending has placed him in the position where he does
not know when he may need his money, and does not know at
what price he may, in such a case, be able to sell his bond. To
lend is to exchange a known for an unknown sum of money. A
lender places himself under a handicap, for which he will
reasonably require insurance and compensation. The terms of
the bond will have to promise a total of payments greater than
the sum which he lends.

How can the degree of compensation for the lender's uncertainty, offered by the terms of a bond, be numerically expressed?

In the expression $P = A_n/(1+r)^n$ let us give the letters the
following meanings:

P   the principal or sum of ready money handed over by the
    lender today;

A_n a one-and-only payment promised by the borrower in
    exchange for the sum lent to him, this payment being due
    after n unit intervals (e.g. years) from today;

n the number of unit intervals' deferment of the borrower's
    sole promised payment;

r a fraction such as one-tenth or one-twentieth, which is
    the 'unknown' to be found by solving our equation.

In this expression, P and A_n and n are all given by the terms of
the bond. The only letter whose numerical value is 'unknown'
until the equation is solved, is r. Having the equation, we can
find a number (in particular, a fraction) to write in place of r,
which will satisfy the equation (make its two sides equal). Then
r will be the rate of discount, or the rate of interest, which the
terms of this bond represent.

The right-hand side of this equation contains only one term,
namely, the payment due after n intervals, reduced by being
divided by a denominator greater than one. But in general,
there will be many such terms, each of the same form as the
one shown, but each assigning a different numerical value to n.
In such a series of terms, the n of our former equation will be
replaced, in the first term by one, in the second term by two,
and so on:

$$P = \frac{A_1}{(1+r)^1} + \frac{A_2}{(1+r)^2} + \ldots + \frac{A_n}{(1+r)^n}.$$

We can still seek a number such that, when written in place of
r, it will make the two sides equal.

Such an expression is very flexible. It can accommodate
many or few terms. The As can be equal or unequal, some of
them can be zero (it will be awkward, mathematically, if some
are negative, but that would be an unusual provision in a bond)
and r can be high (say, $\frac{1}{3}$) or low (say, $1/40$). To say that some
As can be zero, is to say that the time-intervals of non-zero
payments can be unequal.

What is the effect of making r *large?*

The effect is that for a given *P*, the *A*s will be large, and the lender's compensation correspondingly high, the borrower's cost of borrowing equally high.

Why should we not treat r *and the* As *as given, and* P *as the unknown?*

We can do so, then *P* becomes the *price of a series of stated deferred payments*. If we then consider two different levels of *r*, with one and the same series of *A*s, the size of *P* will be larger when *r* is at the lower of the two levels. A lowering of the interest-rate which we are using to discount a given series of deferred instalments increases the value which that series as a whole has at the moment from which we look forward to it. That value is called the *discounted value* of the series at that moment. When that moment is, for some business man, the moment of deciding whether or not to buy the bond, that moment is for him 'the present', and it is natural from this point of view to call the discounted value the *present value* of the series of deferred instalments.

What, in sum, does this equation tell us?

It invites us to see an interest-rate as a reflection of the *price of a series of promised deferred payments*. A price, if it has general and public validity, is something determined ('brought to a particular level') in a market. The interest-rate is determined in the bond-market, and when we ask what influences press upon an interest-rate, the answer is that the list of such influences includes everything that can affect any choice of conduct made by anyone anywhere in the economic world, since any such choice of conduct can press, upwards or downwards, powerfully and closely or remotely and faintly, the prices of bonds and the interest-rates which are arithmetically linked to them. The bond-market is the gathering-point of all the streams of influence which converge upon the interest-rate. The interest-rate is determined in the bond-market. To say so is to place no limitation whatever on the kinds of source, impulse, consideration, conjecture, action or event that can affect the interest-rate.

The interest-rate reflects the price of bonds, and also the price of loans ('sums lent'). How can this be?

To buy a bond, whether from the original borrower whose promise it is, or from the first lender, or from someone who bought it from him, and so on, is to *lend money*. Bond-buying, and lending, are the same act, since it matters nothing to a lender whether he buys a 'new' or a 'second-hand' bond, if the series of promised payments still outstanding is the same for both.

What influences work in the bond-market?

The bond-market differs in three essential ways from a market for perishable fruit. First, it is a market for speculative counters which are not used up or worn out, and which exist in large permanent masses. Secondly, its price-movements can raise or lower the 'steam-pressure' in society's economic boiler. And thirdly, its operations are of high concern to the government, which makes it an object and instrument of policy.

In a market for, let us say, strawberries, the demand from each buyer is for so-and-so much for today's needs, and the supply from each producer is so-and-so much from today's production. The price is governed by the relative strength of the need to buy for today's consumption and the need to dispose of today's production. With such goods, a reserve or store may be technically impossible. In the bond-market, the 'reserve', the stock of bonds which exists all the time, is far larger in relation to the quantity of new bonds offered for sale, or of old bonds redeemed and cancelled, in a time-interval of given length, than the reserve of perishable goods can be to the production of an equal interval. Yet that stock of 'old' bonds can be put on the market, in smaller or larger quantity, at any time. It looms always over the market in some degree.

The price of bonds is not raised by a strengthened need for bonds to 'use up', since they are not used up. It is not even raised chiefly by a strengthened desire for bonds to store away, to add to the stock-pile in somebody's portfolio. The desire for bonds is strengthened chiefly by the spread of a belief that the price of bonds is about to go up. For if this is justified, it will pay to buy bonds today and sell them when the price has risen. What can give rise to such a belief? The catalogue would be endless, the apparent relation between many of its items and the change of bond-prices would be elusive and tenuous, some such links would be those of purely cynical manipulation by interested parties. The bond-market is a *speculative* market. Speculation is a game where knowledge, in the nature of things, is a few islands in an ocean of un-knowledge. We know something about the situation which exists in our 'present moment', we see glimpses of what it may become in the immediate future, the rest is a free field for figment and unreasoned hope or anxiety. Where there is, and can be, no *knowledge* there are signs and portents, omens, the drawing-up of magic charts and the waiting upon auguries, the watching of 'resistance levels', hopes hauling themselves up by their own bootstraps. Movements of prices, up or down, are in large measure self-engendering. Speculation cannot thrive on a price which stays put. Anything that comes to hand will be used to start it rolling. But a movement once started seems to have meaning and continuity of its own. Many who never thought of buying will climb on the band-wagon and give it extra momentum. But there will be constraints. A convention, a generally accepted idea, that bond-prices do not usually go above a certain level or fall below another particular level, will give pause to potential buyers or sellers as the price approaches either of those levels. The pressure to buy will weaken as the upper conventional limit is approached, this weakening will slow down, or stop, the rise, and the 'conventional limit' will have exercised its authority and strengthened it. There is no calculating the impending movements of a speculative market, for any such power would be self-destructive. Those who had such power would use it, and in that act destroy the basis of it. We must not be misled by the advertisements in the financial press. No financial adviser can give advice which will enable *every* reader of his column to buy at the bottom and sell at the top, *every time*. For every buyer at the bottom, there is necessarily a seller at the bottom. Speculation is a 'zero-sum game', what one man gains, another loses, broadly speaking.

How does the bond-price, or its counterpart the interest-rate, stimulate or depress business as a whole?

Is it worth while to start a business? This question suggests two others to start with: What are the things to be compared? What is the nature of those things?

The things to be compared are the expenses in which the business will involve the business man, and the revenues which he expects from it. Each of these categories must be made more exact. We can divide the expenses into the *first cost* of equipment and the *operating expenses* of equipment. To view matters in this way is to direct attention centrally to the equipment, viz. the premises, plant and tools, all of them durable and expensive, as both the receptacle of inputs and the source of revenues. The equipment must be bought or built, then operated. To buy or build equipment is to lay out money in *enterprise investment*. Will the business give back this money? It will, if in each future month or year, to which the business man looks forward at the moment of deciding whether or not to start the business, the proceeds of selling its product are going to exceed by a large enough margin the expense in that month or year for the services of work people, and the materials, needed to operate the equipment. That excess (positive or negative) is an instalment of *trading revenue*. It is a *dated* instalment of trading revenue. The business will be a success if the trading revenues which it will yield, when each is adjusted for the fact of its *deferment*, are going to add up to not less than the first cost of the equipment.

59

What is the nature of these instalments of trading revenue?

They are figments of imagination, hypotheses (suppositions) invented by the business man, they are *thoughts*. What else can they be? They are not 'facts of observation', for there are no eye-witnesses of the future. They are not irrefutable logical consequences deduced from complete evidence, for evidence concerns the past, not the future. The evidence that seems to bear on the future is fragmentary, elusive, confused, even conflicting. Concerning any one future calendar-interval (month or year) the business man in the nature of things is bound in principle to entertain many distinct and rival hypotheses of the size and sign (positive or negative, loss or gain) of the trading revenue of his proposed business in that named interval. This spread or fan of hypotheses will not extend limitlessly on either side of zero. It will be bounded by considerations of what is compatible with the world's capabilities and potentialities as far as the business man can envisage them. But 'the instalment of trading revenue' associated with any future month, if clearly formulated, will be a skein of hypotheses (*suggested* answers to the question 'What will it be?') to each of which some degree of possibility is adjudged.

We have made demands on the reader's attention in aid of this idea, because it is a reflection, in economic subject-matter, of a facet of the Scheme of Things itself. But somehow we must exact from it a sufficient concession to the needs of theory. The crudest of such concessions is to suppose the business man to make, for each future calendar-interval, a 'best guess' as to what the trading revenue of that interval will be. The meaning of 'best guess' can be the figure he would name, if he were offered a prize for naming the right figure. When a series of such figures has been formed, one for each of the calendar-intervals in the supposable life of the equipment, this series will be in one aspect a *series of deferred payments*. A bond-price, as we have seen, is the market price of a different kind of series of deferred payments. The deferred payments of a bond are *promises*. The instalments of trading revenue of a business are conjectures. But both series are series of *deferred* supposed instalments. We saw that a lowering of the interest-rate increases the discounted value of a series of given deferred instalments. If, then, the business man's best guess of the series of trading revenues his proposed business will bring him consists of instalments each greater than zero, a lowering of the interest-rate will increase the valuation he puts on these instalments as a whole, at the moment of making his decision for or against setting up the business. If the first cost of setting up the business is the same for both levels of the interest-rate, his *inducement to make the enterprise-investment* in the business is stronger at the lower interest-rate.

Why must a business man discount his supposed future trading revenues at the rate of interest prevailing in the market for loans of money?

He must do so for his own advantage. If the use of his money to buy a bond will give him a better series of deferred instalments than the use of it to buy a business, it will seem better to buy the bond. The proper comparison between bond and business is the discounted value of their respective series of supposed deferred payments. The discounting must be done at one and the same interest-rate for both, and this interest-rate can only be the one determined in the bond-market, for that is the only one which can apply to bonds.

Is the best guess the only, or the most efficient, way of reducing a skein of rival trading-revenue hypotheses to a manageable form?

No. There are more discriminating and more psychically congruous ways of mapping a skein of hypotheses on to a simpler frame. This we shall examine below.

8

ENTERPRISE-INVESTMENT

What is enterprise?

Enterprise is action in pursuit of imagination. Our being is in a solitary moment. Thought, feeling, decision, action, are *now*, in the solitary present. But they do not *envisage* only the present. We conceive other moments, and regard this conception as entailed by the experienced nature of the present, which exists by transforming itself into a different moment. Our concern in the present is largely with those moments which are still to be. What do we know of them? By direct, eye-witness observation, nothing. By rigid inference from present circumstances, nothing. For how could we know that we have brought into the reckoning all those circumstances which bear on the problem? How can we know that present circumstances can lead only to one course of future history? Why should we assume that the course of events is determined by its past? Is decision itself illusory, the mere determinate, sole possible response of creatures governed by tastes, circumstance and reason? If decision means, what our ways of speech suggest, a *source* of new strands in the texture of events, then if there are to be decisions in future we cannot know their consequences now. Future time is a void which, essentially, we can fill only with imagination.

This is not to say that we can fill it with pure unconstrained and wanton fantasy. Men are protected by a *practical conscience*, which bids them conceive only such sequels to their present action as are congruous with the way they have seen the world to work, and to envisage for given future dates only such situations (states of affairs) as there is time for the world to attain from its present situation, by transformations which seem possible in speed and extent.

Enterprise is conduct by which a man deliberately forgoes the assurance that some particular bad thing will not happen, in order to escape the *certainty* that some particular good thing will not happen. A man who makes a bet destroys the assurance that he will not lose money in a particular way. But he also destroys the certainty that he will not gain money in a particular way. Enterprise differs from a bet in two essential ways. It is not a zero-sum game, for besides the gain of one man which is the loss of the other, there is created some desirable qualities of things, some value is added to what previously existed. And secondly, in enterprise the role of thought and effort, and their leverage upon the outcome, is usually far greater. Enterprise is indispensable, betting is otiose. Yet they have the essential property in common, they represent an endeavour to widen the range of sequels of the present, which can be envisaged without absurdity.

By what tests can a business enterprise, which is in contemplation, commend itself?

The test is its effect on the business man himself, when in imagination he places himself in the position of having committed his means (his own wealth or part of it, the wealth of others which he may persuade them to entrust to him) to buying the necessary equipment to launch the enterprise. Is there some degree of success which seems possible, whose possibility is assented to by his own practical conscience in a sufficient degree, such as to outweigh the corresponding possibility of disaster or misfortune? (To outweigh it in the *scales of his own state of mind*, to make him, in his balancing of anticipations, content?) Are there hopes and anxieties, the latter imposing themselves as the price of the former, which the enterprise would engender in him, and which together would constitute a *good state of mind*? For the only thing the business man can get by committing himself to an enterprise, by opening the door to sequels which, at his moment of decision, are only things conceived in thought, is a state of mind. At his moment of decision, the enterprise itself is a thought and thoughts are all it can provide. His decision must be made on the basis of thoughts and the test of the enterprise lies in his own mind. A decision is made at some moment, and all that bears upon it, all the things that influence it, must be thoughts that occur and exist at that moment.

If the business man is supposed to entertain,
for some contemplated enterprise, a degree of success
and a degree of possibility of that degree of success,
is there not in principle
an infinity of such pairs which he might entertain?

Yes, and each of the two components will help to give, or to withhold, from such a pair its ascendancy in relation to other pairs. The greater the degree of abstract success, considered without regard to its possibility, the more interesting and arresting the idea will be; but the less this degree is assented to as possible, by practical conscience, the less will be its ascendancy. Beyond some point, success greater in the abstract will seem less possible, will entail a greater degree of disbelief. And at some point, growing disbelief as the accompaniment of growing suppositious success, will begin to depress the ascendancy of the pair as a whole. At this point of balance the two influences taken together will define a focus-point, the focus-gain or representative of what the enterprise promises at best. By an argument whose form mirrors the one which defines a focus-gain, we can define a focus-loss. Focus-gain and focus-loss are respectively what the business promises and what it threatens. And they are the products of the judgement of the business man, the product of his thought. To use the fashionable jargon, they are subjective. An enterprise in contemplation does not offer its outcome as an observable fact, for that fact is in the future, beyond the eye of men.

We compared an enterprise, in one of its aspects, to a bet. The notions of focus-gain and focus-loss are the formal expression of that analogy.

What formal calculation defines the gain or loss from the setting-up of an enterprise?

This gain, which we may call the investment gain, is the result of subtracting the first cost of the equipment (premises, plant, tools, initial inventories of materials) from the total of discounted supposed trading revenues. It sounds simple and exact, it may even sound as though the answer would be 'a fact'. No appearances could be more illusory. The entire calculation rests upon imaginative judgement. First cost might be reasonably taken as known, since tenders could be invited. But trading revenues are facets of the unobservable, un-inferable future, they are figments, no matter how thorough and exhaustive the search for data offering suggestions concerning these quantities, no matter with what subtlety the data are combined and analysed. The formal expression of the uncertainty in which the business man is thus irremediably involved, which faces him in the nature of things and is an aspect and illustration of men's essential and eternal predicament, is that he must entertain a number of *rival* hypotheses concerning the series of trading revenues to be associated with a specified outfit of equipment and a specified organization for using it. We have briefly examined two ways in which such a skein of rival answers to a single question can be made manageable for the purpose of decision. As the previous chapter suggested, the business man can be assumed to select from the skein a 'best guess', and substitute this for the range of what seem to him possible answers. Or he can derive focus-points, namely, a focus-gain and focus-loss, as legs upon which the system of hypotheses can in some sense be said to rest.

How can rival enterprise-schemes be compared by means of pairs of focus-outcomes?

Amongst rival proposed enterprises, all those can be eliminated which entail *both* a larger focus-loss and a smaller focus-gain than some one other of the rivals. From those which are left, there will be found a number whose focus-loss is *the greatest tolerable*, in view of the business man's resources. And amongst this further sub-set, there will perhaps be one, or perhaps several, which offer the largest focus-gain. If there is only one member of this third sub-set, that should surely be his choice. If there are several, he will have to look to some second-rank quality or character to decide between the equal front-runners.

What considerations, then, enter into the inducement to invest?

These considerations are thoughts, and they exist and operate in men's minds. The meaning of a concept is nowadays (following P. W. Bridgeman) said to reside in our manner of measuring it. But what we are interested in, in our present context, is the stream of investment itself, the total effect of the various inducing or deterring influences. And any attempt to measure the inducement to invest must really consist in measuring that stream itself. Before we list the influences, we must ask:

Why do we call investment a stream?

Investment has another aspect besides that seen by the investing business man. The investing business man, the enterpriser, buys equipment. But from the point of view of other business men, the equipment is their product. These products form part of the general production of goods of all sorts performed by the society, and that production is an activity, something going on from moment to moment and day by day. When this activity has a given intensity, when a given number of people with given outfits of tools are engaged in it, more production will be done, more value will be added, in a week than in an hour. Production is a flow, a quantity measured as so-and-so many units *per unit of time*. The production of equipment for sale to investing business men as such is part of general production, and must similarly be treated as a flow.

What is the list of investment-influences?

If we formalize the business man's investment-thoughts by means of focus-points, we can say that any piece of news, any item of evidence or any suggestion put into words from any source, which leads him to reduce the *degrees of disbelief* he attaches to the supposition of large trading revenues from his contemplated enterprise, or increase his disbelief in large losses, will push him towards investing in it. A lowering of the interest-rate, or rates, at which the bond-market dictates that supposed trading revenues of future years should be discounted, will raise the present value of any given series of instalments, providing they are positive in algebraic sign. If they were all negative, the present value of these *losses* would be *numerically* increased. But an expected series of trading losses would in itself be a discouragement to investment. If positive and negative suppositious trading revenues are interspersed, we have a complex situation whose response to changes of interest-rate depends on the distribution of these outcomes. Thirdly, there is the matter of the prices of specific pieces of equipment, governing the first cost of setting up an enterprise of given technological design. If this first cost rises, it will plainly weaken the inducement to invest offered by any given system of suppositions about trading revenues and associated degrees of disbelief. Investment-gain is a complex, subtle and elusive idea, not because of any indolence in formulating it, but in its essential nature, and in the nature of the Scheme of Things.

How do investment-decisions fit into the scheme of decisions the business man must make?

His decisions are bound to be exceedingly many and various. For they involve technological detail, the arts and sciences which constitute or underlie his trade. The business man has a profession, and its exercise consists, like that of a physician or a lawyer, in an endless series of acts of resolving questions for which there are insufficient data. The headings under which the economist can classify the business man's perpetual pre-occupations are a mere filing-system composed of broad categories. He must decide, in regard to some impending calendar-interval, how much of his product to produce, that is, what is to be, at stated prices, the amount of his intended *value-added* in this coming interval; what shall be, at stated prices, the value of the goods he will sell at the end of the interval (we suppose, for convenience, that he sells nothing until its end); what shall be, at stated prices, the value of the purchases he will make, at the end of the interval (again for convenience of formulation, we suppose him to buy nothing in the meanwhile) of producers' goods from other firms; and the contracts he shall now make for work to be done for him, by work people whom he now engages or whose employment he continues, during the interval. If

s stands for intended value of sales,

v stands for intended value added,

then $s-v$ stands for the extent to which sales will draw upon his initial inventory to supplement his intended 'value-added',

i stands for his intended value of goods to be bought from other firms,

then $i_n = i - (s-v)$ is his *intended net investment* for the interval.

Here s, v, i and i_n are all of them quantities measured in (i.e. numbers representing) values expressed in money. They must therefore all assume a particular and self-consistent set of prices. In regard to those prices, we have to answer the question

What if the market refuses to buy the assumed
physical quantity of product at the assumed price,
or to supply the assumed physical quantities of
producers' goods at the assumed prices?

There are here two questions. First, what happens to our measurements, if the prices on which they are based (prices *assumed* by the business man) are not validated *ex post* by the market? Then, we shall be reminded (and we ought never to forget) that economics is a discipline from which, by its nature, imprecision and vagueness can never be eradicated. Economics is the science of imprecision.

Secondly, what happens to the business man's formulated policy, his contingent investment-plans for intervals beyond the immediate one? They will have to be revised. The necessity for such revision was recognized by the Stockholm School in the late 1920s and early 1930s, in the concept invented by Gunnar Myrdal of supposing the business man to compare, at the end of each interval, what the book-keeping record declares to have happened 'in fact' with what he envisaged for that interval when he stood upon its threshold.

If the buying and production of equipment
(industrial facilities of all kinds) is only a part of
the whole business of producing goods and
using them to make life possible and enjoyable, why have
we spent a whole chapter on its consideration?

The reason is that though investment is only a part of production, it is a very specially vital part, for the reasons, first, that it provides money incomes without directly providing *consumers' goods* on which they can be spent; and secondly, because it improves and enlarges society's productive power, in a sense which, in common and in character with the rest of economics, is meaningful though imprecise.

9

SAVING, OR NON-CONSUMPTION

What becomes of income?

Income is production. It is the value added in a unit interval of time to an initial collection of goods, in the transformation of that initial collection into another collection by the activity of those whose income we are considering. Their contributions to this transformation may be the work of their brains or hands, or the giving of the use of their possessions. The technological result of their activity takes a thousand or a million different forms. These forms cannot themselves be directly added together. Yet income is a single number. To make them addable, the technological results must be valued. Thus we think of income as a sum of money related to an interval of time.

What use is money income?

It is handed over to the contributors to production, to symbolize their ownership of the results of production. They claim those results by buying them with the money. What happens if they do not, between them, buy all of the results? What happens if those results, or some of them, have to be sold to them for less than the money income which was given to them in exchange for their productive services? And as a means of insight into these questions, we may ask

Why do the contributors to production buy the products? Or why do they refrain from buying them?

They buy some of them in order to live. They buy much of them in order to enjoy living. But many of them do not spend the whole of their incomes on maintaining or enjoying life. The rest they use to build up a collection of assets, a collection of particular forms of wealth. These can comprise money itself, or bonds, the acknowledgements and promises of a borrower, or the shares of companies, or tangible objects such as buildings and machines. In so far as incomes are paid to them for making things which they do not buy as consumers, as people needing food, fuel, clothes, entertainment, what happens to those things which are produced in a named week or year but are not matched by similar or equivalent things consumed in that same week or year? Those things which are produced over and above what is needed to make good contemporaneous consumption are necessarily added to the stock-pile of wealth. But there are two ways in which they may be so added: by the deliberate action of those who fit them into a scheme of production of other goods, who use them in their enterprises; or by contrast, through being left in the hands of those who had expected to sell them (in effect) to consumers, but have been disappointed in that hope. In Chapter 8 we saw that goods bought for improving and enlarging the productive power of business as a whole are part of the stream of new production. The question that obviously presents itself is

How is business men's demand for equipment to improve their productive power related to income receivers' desire to build up their personal wealth?

To ask this is to ask two questions: How are the two things related in *quantity* and in *motive*? If the buying of assets by income-receivers is part of their policy for disposing of their incomes, we may expect their monthly, yearly (*et cetera*) purchase of such assets to be related in value to the size of their aggregate income. We must of course distinguish between the total monthly or yearly value of the sales and purchases of assets, on the Stock Exchange, the property market, and so on, which will always include a huge volume of 'second-hand' sales, on one hand; and the monthly or yearly value of newly-produced or newly-created assets, on the other; and amongst these latter we must distinguish between documents (bonds, debentures, money) and the physical, technological tools whose making is a part of production. These apparent complexities, however, are for our purpose more daunting than they need be. What we are concerned with is the comparison of the gap between incomes and consumption-spending, on one hand, with the ordering and buying of equipment for enlarging society's productive power, on the other. For if those two were in some way guaranteed to be, in each unit interval of time, *equal* to each other, an essential theoretical and a vital practical problem would be resolved. The production not required by consumers would, in that case, find *willing and deliberate* buyers amongst business men in their capacity, not as private individuals wanting goods for sustenance and enjoyment, but as enterprise investors.

But will these two things be equal or unequal?
What could bring them towards equality?

These two quantities, as they exist in people's minds at the threshold of any particular, named interval (say, January 1973) to which they refer, will each be the result and the expression of a set of decisions made independently of the set of decisions which governs the other. The term 'independently' needs some qualification, but it essentially conveys the truth. Those whom we have called 'contributors to production' and 'income-receivers' and who for our immediate purpose are to be thought of as income-*disposers*, compose a class which includes, as a sub-class, the business men who initiate, direct and organize production. But the class and the sub-class are not merely partly independent as classes: each member of each class is, in general and in the main, uninformed of the concurrent decisions of the other individuals. As a disposer of his own supposed income, a business man takes decisions which can call upon the same sources of suggestion and the same evidence (fragmentary or ostensibly coherent, sparse or rich) as his decisions concerning enterprise-investment, but it would be the sheerest accident if the two quantities, his intended saving out of income and his intended purchase of equipment, should for the impending interval be equal. (And we have to remember that in any such argument as this, 'the business man' is a composite of a firm's chief executive, its board and its shareholders at large.) And if his own intended saving and his own intended enterprise-investment are not equal, it is certain that his knowledge of other people's intentions in these two regards is negligible and cannot by any manner of means enable him to fit together a jig-saw puzzle in which, as a whole, the society's aggregate intended saving would be equal to its aggregate intended enterprise-investment. There is no organization and no means by which the two sets of intentions are or can be *pre-reconciled*. They are essentially mutually independent, their equality, if by some chance it should occur, would indeed be the result of chance.

If the society's aggregate intended enterprise-investment and its aggregate intended saving, are only equal by accident, what is the importance of their relation?

It is the two aggregates of *intentions*, the two quantities assigned to the interval at its threshold, *ex ante*, that are unconstrained to equality. When the end of the interval shall have been reached, and its record is available, the two *ex post* quantities, the excess, on the one hand, of production over consumption, and the excess, on the other hand, of income over spending on consumption, must by the meaning we give to these terms be equal. Thus, then, between pairs of intended quantities which are (except by remote chance) unequal, and realized quantities which are equal, there must be some adjustment. It is in the need for this adjustment, and the manner in which it comes about, that the course of business, the economic history of the society in regard to the size of its general output and the level of its employment, is determined.

73

How can the ex post *quantities come to equality?*

If intended aggregate saving (non-spending on consumption) exceeds aggregate intended outlay on enterprise-investment, the part of production which is unsold for consumption will not be wholly bought for investment. But since the part which is not wanted either by consumers or investors will nonetheless have been produced, it must remain in the hands of its producers as an *unwanted* accretion to their stock-piles of goods. There will have been some *unintended* investment. This outcome of the total set of decisions, for production, investment, and income disposal, taken by individual persons or interests at the beginning of the interval, will not become apparent until its end. But that end is the beginning of a new interval. What will be the effect of the divergence of the former *ex ante* quantities upon the new set of decisions which must now be taken concerning the new forthcoming interval?

Does this question carry us beyond the reach of demonstration into that of conjecture?

It does, and our only proper business, as analysts, is to point out that there is in this type of divergence a source of influence on decisions and thus a 'source of history'. The kind of conjecture which will suggest itself is readily apparent. We may take it as likely that producers who find themselves with goods on their hands which they had expected to sell will be tempted to reduce their output for the immediate future. But this guess takes no account of the many explanations of the recent short-fall of demand, which producers may now perceive and may regard as unlikely to be repeated. The engenderment of history is complex and subtle beyond penetration.

What are the policy lessons of this scheme of thought?

The lesson concerns unemployment, and what is implied if there is to be full employment. For the way of looking at things which we have outlined (and it is J. M. Keynes's way in his *The General Theory of Employment, Interest and Money*) indicates that full employment, in order to be sustainable, requires the saving gap between full employment output and consumption-spending by those whose incomes in total represent that output, to be filled by the spending of those who want goods for other purposes than consumption. Of these other purposes, the most important in principle (since it applies to a closed economy such as the world as a whole) is enterprise-investment in a wide sense. This 'enterprise'-investment may be performed by the 'private sector' of firms which are in business on their own account; or by publicly-owned corporations; or by governments, local or central. Other contributory streams of demand for products may come, in an 'open' economy such as that of Britain which trades with an outside world, from exporters in our country, who buy goods to sell overseas. Such exports do not directly absorb any of the spending of our own income-disposers, though the exports may be offset or more than offset by imports which do absorb our consumers' spending.

What is the shorthand language for handling these ideas?

The proportion of any increment of their aggregate income, which income-disposers as a body spend on goods for immediate consumption or personal use, was called by Keynes the *marginal propensity to consume*. In mathematical terms this is the derivative of aggregate consumption with respect to aggregate income, when the former is looked on as a function (in the mathematical sense) of the latter; that is to say, when spending is looked on as varying, in a way which we can reduce to a formal quantitative rule, under the governance of income. What Keynes neglected, the question he failed to ask himself, was whether the income and the spending in question are *intentions* or *realizations*. As a consequence his argument was elliptical, and obliterated the possibility of asking how the process of adjustment of intentions to each other comes about.

Keynes's phrase *the propensity to consume* admirably suggests

75

the heart of the matter. It has subsequently become usual to speak instead of the *consumption-function*.

Does the size of the intended, or the realized, saving-flow really depend only on the size of related income?

Of course this would be a drastic simplification. But 'drastic' does not mean 'unjustified'. For all theory is simplification, otherwise it would be pointless. A theory involving as much detail and complexity as the object being studied would be worthless, since it would be as hard to grasp as the object, but without the same claim to be true.

10

EMPLOYMENT

*If people always feel a desire for larger supplies of things,
or for faster improvement of their equipment,
why do they not always remain* fully employed
in productive activities?

To gain insight into this question, we need the answers to two
others: What is *full employment?* What considerations or influences govern the level of employment which prevails at any
time?

A person will be fully employed when the reward of an
extra hour's work, beyond the weekly hours he is already doing,
would not compensate him for the loss of an hour's leisure. If
so, how can anyone ever fail to get himself fully employed?
Can he not offer his services at a low enough price to make it
worth someone's while to employ him up to the number of
weekly hours that this price determines as full employment for
him? The Theory of Value and Distribution, that is, the
equilibrium theory of universal pre-reconciliation of choices,
would say that involuntary unemployment is a contradiction
in terms, or is in the nature of things impossible. It would argue
on the lines we have just suggested.

Since it has been possible in this century in Britain for a
million or more people to be out of work, who would gladly
work for the current wages of those who are in work, or for less,

*What is the fallacy in the view taken by
the equilibrium theory?*

Let us first be more exact about the equilibrium theory. In this
theory, what are incomes paid in? They are paid in products,

in the goods themselves that income-receivers collaboratively make and that are desired for their own sake, to consume or to use as tools. If you are paid in products, you have to make up your mind what products, in what quantities, you will accept in exchange for this or that weekly quantity of work, or of use of your property, and so on. Each extra hour added to your weekly hours may seem more expensive in the rest and recreation it robs you of. But the quantity of goods produced by your extra hour will not increase as the total of weekly hours, to which this hour is added, mounts up. If some one factor of production (working space, tillable fields, specialized plant) are, for the time being, fixed in quantity, the product of an extra hour may even decline as the hours get longer. There will be a point of balance, where the product of an extra hour is just and only just enough to compensate the extra weariness. When this point has been found, and applied, for everyone, that will be a state of full employment. At that point, no employer will wish to give less employment, for to do so would lose him more in reduced production than it would save him in wages. No employer will wish to give more employment, for to do so would cost him more in wages, paid in product, than the product it would yield him. Full employment, by its meaning within the frame of the equilibrium theory, is a *naturally* attained, and maintained, position.

> *Is there something special about the assumptions of the equilibrium theory, on which its implication of full employment depends?*

Yes. It makes every contributor to production, every income-receiver, an enterprise-investor, it abolishes the distinction between employers and employed. In describing the equilibrium theory, we have spoken of 'employers'. But the situation and duty of such employers would be different from those in a *money-using* economy. In the equilibrium economy, there is not a class of people who shoulder all the risks of enterprise, by deciding what shall be produced before they can know whether or not it will successfully sell. Equilibrium is that state of affairs, that aspect of a particular organization of affairs, where the problem of how knowledge of circumstance is to be attained has been solved. People are assumed to know what goods they want. Or, at any rate, they have, all of them, to decide what goods they want. The meaning of *full employment* includes a special meaning for the pay of an extra weekly hour. That pay, being in product, must be sufficient to compensate for loss of leisure *despite any uncertainty about the usefulness of the product.*

How is this situation different from that of a money-using economy?

Money is what allows you *to put off deciding what to buy.* In a money-using economy there can exist, distinct from other economic performers, the *enterpriser-employer,* a class of people who alone decide what things shall be made, the society at large being left to decide whether to buy what has been made, or not. It follows that the question, what is the marginal, the *extra,* weekly hour of work, added to some given number of hours, worth to the employer, is something which he must guess, something which he cannot *know* until after he has given this employment. In a non-money-using society, everyone would share these uncertainties, the uncertainties would be subsumed into the general question: How distasteful is one extra hour of employment? This extra hour would be distasteful, partly because it would involve loss of leisure, because it would involve the experience of effort instead of relaxation; but partly also because the reward of these disabilities would be an unknown benefit, the benefit of acquiring things for use in the unknown circumstances of the future, things which might turn out extremely desirable or entirely useless. In the money economy, the bearing of these uncertainties can be specialized to a particular group, the enterprise-producers and enterprise-investors. The value of a marginal hour's employment can thus seem higher to the *potential employed person* than to the potential employer, and the unemployment or under-employment of the former can thus seem 'involuntary'.

What could the potential employed, the people seeking jobs or longer weekly hours, do to make this extra employment seem worth the employers' while to give?

To offer their services, their productive contribution, at lower money wages or other money pay, will not serve, since if their spending out of one level of money income would not suffice to buy the product of their work, their spending out of a lower level of income would perhaps be no more able to buy it, even though its wage-cost had thus become less. But if the income-receivers all taken together (and they include the employers) could accept a differently-composed collection of products as the reward of their combined efforts, this different composition of the product might reduce the uncertainty felt by the employers concerning its value sufficiently for the employers to give more employment. In what precise way would that composition need to be altered? The total product would have to consist more largely of goods looking for use in the near or immediate future, where uncertainty is least, and less of goods looking to distant years. It would have to consist more largely of consumers' goods and less of enterprise-investment.

How, precisely, would such a change in the time-orientation of the general total product work to reduce the employer-enterprisers' hesitation to produce?

It would work partly by reducing the uncertainty concerning the usefulness of the product, making this usefulness to rest on near-future envisaged uses rather than on remote-future uses; and partly by transferring some of the burden of uncertainty remaining, to the shoulders of employed persons, requiring them to accept some 'goods useful in themselves' instead of some of the general purchasing power they would perhaps have preferred. What seems needed, then, is an organized possibility for potential-employed people to trade off unemployment against uncertainty: to accept some uncertainty in exchange for being freed of some unemployment.

How would such a change in the composition of the society's aggregate product-income be expressed in conventional terms?

It would be described as a higher propensity to consume making good an insufficient flow of enterprise investment. When the society's aggregate demand for products, the aggregate spending by the income-receivers on the goods they collaborate in producing, has to consist too much in spending by business men on improving and enlarging their distant-looking equipment, and too little on goods for immediate enjoyment, if there is to be full employment, this full employment will fail to be attained. The necessary flow of spending on improvement of equipment will be inhibited by too great uncertainty. The cure can come in the weakening of this uncertainty, some change in the thoughts which 'the news' suggests to business men; or it can come from a decrease in the proportion of its money income which society tries to save, a reduction (at any given level of this aggregate income) of the saving-gap which has to be filled by enterprise-investment.

What are the consequences of the dependence of employment on enterprise-investment?

They arise from the dependence of enterprise-investment on a state of mind, including the suggestions which each mind has (recently) received, i.e. 'the news', and the use it has made of them, the *imaginative construction* it has put upon them. For the suggestions offered by 'the news' are fragments scarcely relatable to each other, and very far from composing, on their own, a coherent or a complete picture. Thus the enterprise-investor, the business man, has very great originative freedom to make them the basis of any expectations his mood encourages. That mood itself will reflect an inscrutable social process: news, interpretations, actions, consequences, fresh derivations of thoughts from those consequences; inter-actions of minds; the rise or collapse of 'confidence'. Enterprise-investment is not a rational response to *circumstances completely known*. It is, on the contrary, an *originative* act, part of a skein of contemporaneous originations by many individuals, which between them *create* in large measure the determining circumstances of their own outcomes.

*If enterprise-investment is at once so important,
and so elusively engendered, and so mutable in size
of aggregate flow, what can be done?*

We mean, what can be done by the government to prevent large changes of the size of flow from upsetting employment and the attainment of prosperity for everyone? In so far as individual business men's or firms' decisions to improve their equipment depend on suggestions, and the diffusion of the resulting outlook, rather than on demonstrative reasoning from established facts, the government can take action which offers such suggestions. It can ensure that expected net trading revenues will seem subject to less heavy taxes, and will be discounted at lower rates of interest, than those which prevail. It can itself act as business man, and give orders (or sanction them) for improvement of the equipment of publicly-owned industries, or of 'social capital' such as roads, hospitals and housing. There is no case for supposing that government cannot *influence* enterprise-investment. There is no case for supposing that it can bring about precisely-measured changes at particular lengths of time ahead of 'the present'. Moreover, a practice of continual attempted control of the pace of private-sector investment will soon destroy its own effectiveness. Investment, of its nature, looks many years ahead. Its apparent worthwhileness therefore depends on expectations, that is, conjectures, concerning a stretch of future years. If changes of the 'climate' are brought about by government action at much shorter intervals than the *investment horizon*, the distance into the future which enterprise-investors look, their belief in any possibility of forming expectations will be destroyed, and with it most of the inducement to invest. Governments cannot have it both ways. If there is a 'private sector' of business, a government must seek to offer a stable, reliable and calculable climate in which enterprise-investment can do its best to exploit the possibilities opened by new knowledge and changing circumstance. If it wishes to use investment as a means of policy, it must take control of the flow of investment in a positive sense, by itself becoming a large enterprise-investor. It may be that a half-and-half economy such as we have in Britain in the 1970s, where a large proportion of industry and commerce is publicly owned, is the best arrangement. It gives the government powerful positive leverage while still giving the originative genius of individuals its openings to great success. But the attempt to have a *controlled private enterprise sector* is muddled thinking and a contradiction in terms. 'Fine tuning' of private sector enterprise-investment is nonsense.

Investment is a lever for lifting or lowering the flow of production as a whole. What gives it this leverage?

Keynes's *General Theory of Employment, Interest and Money* has two broad aspects. Let us compare society in its enterprise-investing capacity to an engine producing a power-output. This engine requires both a source of energy (its fuel) and a means of turning this energy into movement. The source of energy is the inducement to invest. The means by which this stimulates production in general, output as a whole, is the mechanical linkages in the engine, its rods, shafts and gears. In the economy, the gearing which multiplies the effect of given increases or decreases in the size of flow of aggregate investment is called the Multiplier. It has been too prominent in discussion of Keynes's theory of employment, for, being just sufficiently mysterious to engage curiosity, and just sufficiently amenable to simplified formulation to make it ostensibly accessible, it has formed a fine parade ground for those who think that economics is a tidy intellectual drill. The original precise formulation of the Multiplier principle by R. F. (Lord) Kahn in 1931 was a great theoretical step, made possible by incisive discarding of inhibitions and by asking the right questions. It gave the *theory of policy* one of its most valuable tools. But Lord Kahn's ingenious revelation of simplicity in the Multiplier principle has helped the defenders of rationalist orthodoxy to divert attention from the other, far more essential, radical and heretical meaning of the *General Theory*, namely, the destruction of the idea of economic society as a setting for wholly rational and rationally analysable conduct and orderly, explainable engenderment of history.

What is the Kahn–Keynes Multiplier?

It is a simple arithmetical consequence of a fractional propensity to consume. If society insists on consuming (destroying for sustenance and enjoyment) only a proper fraction k of its aggregate general output, then the larger that output, the larger will be the saving gap. The larger the intended aggregate flow of net investment (the larger the aggregate of intentions), the larger the saving gap which can be filled. Since extra output ($\equiv$ income) will be only partly saved, only part of it need be offset by extra investment, and extra investment must be *multiplied* (by a number greater than one) to find its corresponding extra general output. If k is the proportion which the society will consume out of any increment of its aggregate income, then $1/(1-k)$ is the Multiplier, the factor by which any difference of two supposable levels of enterprise-investment would have to be multiplied to find the corresponding increment of general output.

Does the Multiplier 'work' instantaneously, as some have said, or does it take time, as Lord Kahn's exposition seemed to imply?

On this question it is no use appealing to Lord Keynes, for in the *General Theory* he makes two incompatible statements in a page or two. The Multiplier works by people's response to the visible effects of other people's actions, therefore it must take time. But it need not by any means proceed through the algebraic series of terms of Lord Kahn's formula at a pace of one term per 'week' or other fixed interval. Lord Kahn's formula is simple. He assumes that at a time of heavy general unemployment, extra workers can be engaged by simply offering them the current rate of money wages, with no need to increase it. The government initiates an extra flow of investment in the form of a road-building programme. The first stage consists in engaging a number of hitherto unemployed men at a total weekly wage of, say, £1 million. The simplest (but too naive) account of the sequel is to suppose that these men will do no extra spending until the end of the week, and will then spend on extra consumption a proportion k of the £1 million of wages they will then receive. Where do the consumption-goods come from, that are bought with this £k million? Again, the simplest account supposes that the instant this extra flow of goods begins to leave the shops, manufacturers of such goods engage a further party of hitherto unemployed men and pay them £k million to make an extra flow of consumers' goods. At the end of a second week, this second party of men will receive their first pay packet of £k million, and *will spend a proportion* k *of it.* But this will necessitate the engagement of a third extra increment of workers, to make a second extra stream of consumption goods, worth k times k million pounds, k^2 million pounds. And so on. Where does the process end? Formally, it does not end. The total of extra weekly wages, towards which the steady week-by-week process of engaging extra workers leads, can be expressed by an infinite series of terms. If we take £1 million as our unit, the number of £millions will be $1 + k + k^2 + k^3 \ldots$, a series extending for ever, but with ever-diminishing successive terms which keep its total within a *limit*. The 'one' represents the weekly £1 million paid to the new road builders themselves. The other terms, k, k^2 and so on, represent the weekly wages of the successively-recruited parties of workers who are to supply extra consumption-goods. A simple manipulation (shown in every algebra book) tells us that if k is a positive proper fraction (a number greater than zero and less than one) the result of adding the terms of an endless series like the above is

$$1 + k + k^2 + \ldots = \frac{1}{1-k}.$$

But if there are endless terms, and only one term is added each week, will it not take endless weeks to get through the series? It would do so, if in fact it took a week for extra employment to result in extra spending. But why should it? A man who is given a job when formerly he had none is better off from the moment when he is engaged. If he is known to have a job, people will be anxious to supply him with the extra goods for which his new job will enable him to pay. The pace at which the series of terms of the Multiplier formula is eaten up does not depend on the mechanical process of receiving coins in a weekly pay-packet and handing them over the counter of a shop. It depends on the pace of diffusion of *ideas*: knowledge or beliefs about what is happening, suggestions, conjectures, decisions to 'get in first' with putting extra supplies on the market. Economics is not concerned with the chatter of the cash register, but with what goes on in men's minds.

How can an increase of employment be encouraged?

It is harder to answer this question than it was when Keynes wrote *The General Theory*. Then he could assume that the money-unit meant, for everyone, the power to purchase constant, or only slowly and moderately changing quantities of staple goods and means of production. Everyone assumed, mostly without conscious thought, that something which could vaguely, but meaningfully, be called money's 'general purchasing power' or 'value in terms of goods' would be as great next year as this year, or even as great in ten years' time as 'today'. Such a money has unique qualities and powers. It has *liquidity*, that elusive and composite but compelling characteristic which gives private consolation at the cost of social inertia.

Money whose future purchasing power is relied on, offers to conserve an individual's or a firm's wealth in a form not exposed to destruction by technical innovation, it can enable him to put off deciding what to buy or what equipment to invest in, it is *general*, non-specific, purchasing power. When there is a general or widespread feeling that circumstances are especially and unusually fluid, many people may wish to resort to money as a store of wealth. They may try to sell their property and equipment in order to hold money instead, money whose value is safe in terms of money. If the result of this is a greater decline in the value of *products* than in that of the *means of production*, if the money prices of goods go down faster than wages, there will be a strong discouragement to production and enterprise. Liquidity preference, finding only a limited existing stock of money to satisfy it, will begin to strangle enterprise and employment. May not the remedy be to increase rapidly the size of society's money stock so that the money price of the assets which people sell does not fall so much? In the 1930s, such a remedy was appropriate. In the early 1970s it is being tried on a massive scale, but in conditions which have been wholly transformed in one essential respect. Money is no longer expected to retain a vaguely but meaningfully 'fixed' purchasing power from this year to the next, from year to future year. On the contrary. A whole generation of people have now seen money prices of goods and of means of production rise continually throughout those people's lives, and latterly with a strong threat of acceleration. Nowadays they assume that this rise will go on, indefinitely, 'for ever'. In 1971 the prices of houses are said to have increased by 20 percent and some, in the first *three months* of 1972, by 7 percent. Are people deciding to 'get out of money into goods'? Money is no longer a safe store of wealth. A massive increase in the size of the nation's stock of money, such as we have been seeing, can help the process of 'inflation' to accelerate to disaster.

INFLATION

What is inflation?

According to the natural scientists, the meaning of a thing is to be found in the way we measure it. Length is what we measure with a foot-rule, density is what we arrive at by dividing the weight of a thing by the weight of an equal volume of water. On these lines, *inflation is what we measure by an index number* of prices in general.

What are prices in general?

They are the prices of some collection of exactly specified goods, so chosen that, when appropriately proportioned to each other in quantity, they represent the regular needs of some wide class of people.

How many distinct collections meeting this description could be found?

An unlimited number. An index number is the answer to a sum, and the data of that sum can be chosen within a wide region and still serve much the same purpose. There is a range of choice, not only in the list of prices to be averaged, but in the procedure for getting the average. It can consist simply in adding together the sums of money required to buy the physical quantities used by a family in a year. When we take this total at the prices of some particular year, called the base year, and represent it by 100, the index number for other years will be got by dividing the total for any such other year by the total of the base year, and expressing the result as a percentage. If the index number of the later year is 150, this is as good an entitlement as any other for saying that 'prices had risen by a half', and as good a meaning as we can assign to the latter statement. Instead of the method we have described, the average of the changes of price of individual goods can be calculated in other ways. The choice of method is in some sense a matter of judgement and even of taste. 'The price level' is a vague phrase of no precise meaning. We cannot give it precision, for it can be represented by any one of an unlimited number of different calculations amongst which the choice is always arguable. Yet the meaning, if not precise, is real, and is necessary to social and political discourse.

What is 'the value of money'?

The value of money is the purchasing power of money over goods wanted for their own sake. That purchasing power will depend on what these goods are, in what proportions they are wanted, and on their prices. It will, that is to say, depend on the same things as an index number of prices in general. Like an index number, it will not be something absolute, but a means of comparing the state of affairs at one date with that at another. If 'the general price-level' doubles between two dates, 'the purchasing power of money' will have halved between those dates, when the price-level and the purchasing-power both refer to the same formula for 'prices in general'.

Why do we speak of 'inflation'?

It is a short expression for 'a general rise of prices'. But it also conveys the idea that there is some special source of this rise, something which is done, or allowed, by 'the monetary authority'. Whatever conduct or policy promotes a general rise of prices is 'inflationary', no matter whose conduct or policy it is. Such a rise may be beyond anyone's control, and it may be even beyond the power of a government to stop, unless that government is determined to stop it *at all costs*. And who knows what those costs would be, in hardship and possible social upheaval? 'Inflation' is not some single identifiable sin of commission or omission, the cessation of which would stop the general rise of prices.

How, then, does inflation occur?

It occurs when the demanders of goods and services offer a larger weekly or annual total of money for them than the weekly or annual quantity of these goods-in-general, which can be produced, is worth at the prevailing prices. This is demand inflation. Or it occurs when those who can supply productive services believe that if they raise the prices of their services, demanders will pay a larger weekly or annual total for them than they are currently paying. This is cost inflation. Like all other economic action, the actions which bring about inflation are induced by beliefs about what their consequences will be. All thoughts, of every kind, suggested by no matter what source in observation, propaganda or ambition, which give hope of advantage to be had by offering, or by asking, higher prices for particular kinds of goods or kinds of service than prevail at the time of these thoughts, are a source promoting 'inflation', or, as we should do well to say, promoting a general rise of money prices. Action arises in thought. And where does thought arise?

Is there a 'mechanism' of inflation?

Is there a regular sequence of effects generated one out of another, through which the original impulse leading eventually to a general rise of prices must exert its influence? We can say that there are some formal frames into which the kinds of events which accompany a general price-rise can be fitted. Some of these merely re-cast the question What causes inflation? into a different and perhaps slightly more specific form. The so-called Quantity Theory of Money pays attention only to those prices which are the terms of actually-recorded trans-actions; that is to say, the terms on which money has actually been given in exchange for goods. If we have some method of giving meaning to the phrase 'the quantity of goods-in-general which changes hands in some interval of time', so that we can tell when this quantity is unchanged, or can tell to what extent it changes, then we can say that a general rise of the prices of these goods, when their quantity is unchanged, ought to be measured in such a way that it implies an increase in the total of money given in exchange for these goods. Why do we need so long and complex a sentence to express the matter? Because 'the matter' is not simple and straightforward, but is one in which the meanings of terms depend on each other, a different choice of one meaning involving a different choice of others. The Quantity Theory of Money really asserts that the notions of quantity of goods, quantity of money, and price-level, can be so defined that they are related by a simple formula.

In the formula $MV = PT$, we can at first regard the two sides as two different ways of arriving at, or of explaining, the total 'money's worth' changing hands during some time-interval; some named calendar week, month or year, or some such interval regarded as typical of a particular stretch of history. MV arrives at this total by taking M, the number of money-units *existing*, and multiplying it by V, the number of times, on the average over all existing units, that such a unit changes hands during the time-interval in question. PT arrives at the total by regarding the entire collection of objects and packets of goods exchanged for money during this interval as so-and-so many 'units of quantity', a number which is then multiplied by the 'average price' of these units of quantity. The formula, thus regarded, expresses a truism: the money given in exchange for goods during a proper named, or during a typical, week or year will be equal to the money-value of goods thus bought.

What can the truism MV $=$ PT *tell us?*

If V, the number of times a unit of money, on the average over all existing units, is exchanged for goods in a year, remains unchanged from year to year, and if the number of 'units of goods' exchanged for money in a year remains unchanged from year to year, then any change, from one year to another, in P, the average price of goods units, must, by mere arithmetic, be accompanied by an equal proportionate change in M the number of existing money units. Thus if M can be increased by administrative action, or if it increases 'of its own accord' by the un-coordinated conduct of individuals, firms and banks, then there will be an accompanying increase of P. The fact that $MV = PT$ is a truism, the fact that it merely offers us two aspects of one and the same measurable thing, does not imply that it can cast no light for us. The mere fact that there are two ways of looking at one set of transactions, the bringing of this contrast and comparison to our notice, does cast such light. But the light it casts merely brings into view further questions.

How does a change come about in the quantity of money in existence?

And first we must ask How do we measure the quantity of money in existence? What counts as money? All definitions in words, of no matter what, are circular. For the words used in a definition must themselves be defined, the words used in these further definitions require still further words, and so on, until we come at last, inevitably, to a definition which depends upon the words we started with. To break into this circle we must have something to point at, or something whose meaning and nature can be taken to be the same for everyone. What role and character are peculiar to money? Is it not the role and character of being accepted in exchange merely because of a belief that it can again be given in exchange to someone else? Such a role we may call *payment*. If we can get everyone to agree that he or she knows when he or she is being paid, to agree that payment is a thing whose occurrence we can all point to, then the notion of payment may serve as our bedrock for defining money. Money is what serves to make payments.

What is money in existence?

Money in existence means money in existence *at some moment*. We must not add together money which exists at 4 p.m. on Monday and money which exists at noon on Tuesday, and say that the total is money in existence. Money which exists, exists simultaneously. Money which exists is money ready at some one moment to make payments, *all of them at once*. We must not count as money, both the pound note in your pocket and the pound note in mine, if they are both the same note before and after it has been given by one of us to the other.

What things can make payments, and can do so purely because of faith that they can be so used again in future?

These things are, in the most obvious place, the 'official' money stamped or engraved with the Sovereign's name or image: coins and Bank of England notes. Any creditor is obliged by law to accept these notes in settlement of any debt, They are *legal tender* money. Secondly, there is the right to require a bank to pay to some third party a sum of legal tender money. What confers such a right? The possession of a bank account which is either in credit, so that the bank is in debt to the holder of the account, or else is allowed by the bank to be drawn upon despite the fact that this will put the holder of the account in debt to the bank. We may say that *money* comprises three kinds of thing: legal tender money; balances owed by banks to non-banks, i.e. to individuals and firms and institutions outside the banking system; and unused permission to overdraw. The *quantity of money in existence at some moment* is the total, at that moment, of legal tender money, credit balances at the banks, and sums which the banks have given their customers permission to add to their existing indebtedness to the banks.

By what operation, then, does the quantity of money in existence increase?

It increases when the banks increase the *further* quantity they are willing to lend. For this must evidently be the first step in any increase of the total of the three components. The quantity of legal tender money in the pockets and tills of the public can only increase if they draw such money out of their bank accounts. These will thus be reduced by the same amount as the circulating notes and coin are increased. The balance owed by a bank to one person or firm can be increased only by transfer from someone else's account, or by a reduction of someone's notes and coins. The only source of extra money is extra lending by the banks. Money, we may say, comes into existence by the creation of mutual indebtedness between the banks and the non-bank part of society. But by far the greatest borrower of money is the government.

What happens when the government borrows money?

The government can borrow money from any of three kinds of lender. In the first place, it can cause money to be created for it by the Bank of England. Over the amount of such creation, there is ultimately no control except by Parliament. Over Parliament there is no control except, at intervals of several years, by the electorate. Government borrowing from the Bank of England can take various forms of various degrees of directness or roundaboutness, but the essential is that a two-sided transaction takes place. The Treasury issues IOUs, and these find their way to the Bank of England in exchange for figures written in the books of the Bank, saying that so-and-so much money is at the disposal of those who brought these 'Treasury Bills' to the Bank.

When the government pays money away to firms and citizens in exchange for the goods and services which government purposes require, these firms and citizens will present the government's cheques to their own banks, and these banks in turn will present them to the Bank of England. Thus the firms and citizens acquire 'credit balances' (money owed to them by their banks) or reduce their own indebtedness to their banks. But the banks themselves will have achieved something more dramatic. They will have acquired balances owed to them by the Bank of England, and standing to their credit in the books of the Bank of England. And these balances count as *cash*.

What if they do count as cash?

There is a limitation on the amount that, in total, the commercial banking system (the system other than the Bank of England) can lend. This limitation is a consequence of the way our money institutions are organized. A good deal of our 'petty' book-keeping is done, not by writing in books or putting data on computer tape, but by handing notes and coins about from one person to another. The handing-about of notes and coins is simply a means of account-keeping. But it is still an integral part of our arrangements. A mass of weekly wages are still paid in notes and coin, and a still larger part of such incomes is spent in notes and coin. As the total quantity of money in existence (of all three kinds taken together) goes up, so will the quantity of notes and coin that the non-bank public desires to have in its pockets and tills. They will go to their banks to draw out this cash, and the banks, if they are to fulfil the understanding on which they borrow money from the public, that is, hold deposits for the public, must be prepared to supply as much cash as the public desire. It follows that when the commercial banks, all taken together, increase the quantity of money in existence by increasing the total amount they are willing to lend, they must have regard to the likely effect, a demand by the public for extra notes and coin, extra 'cash'.

Where can the extra cash come from?

Ultimately, from the Bank of England. The ordinary banks, where the public have their accounts, have accounts themselves at the Bank of England. And the money standing to their credit in the books of the Bank of England *counts as cash*. It follows that when the government increases its debt to the Bank of England, and pays this extra borrowed money away to the public, it increases the power of the ordinary banks to lend money to the public.

What is the sequence of events?

Essentially, it is simple. The government gives IOUs to the Bank of England, which gives the government the right to pay away money to the public, by writing cheques on the Bank of England. The public pays these cheques into its accounts at the commercial (the ordinary) banks, which pay them into their accounts at the Bank of England. The commercial banks now have extra elbow-room to lend money. For the thing which ultimately limits the amount they can lend, is that every such extra loan makes a deposit equal to itself, or reduces someone's overdraft and restores to him his 'unused permission to over-draw'. And when a person's or a firm's available cheque-writing power is increased in either of these two ways, he will ordinarily use some of it to draw out some extra cash. He will use *some proportion* of his extra available money to take out extra cash. It will be quite a small proportion; on the average of firms and persons everywhere, far less than half. And that means that each extra million pounds standing to the credit of the commercial banks, in the books of the Bank of England, increases their lending power by many millions.

But cannot prices be raised if we have a faster-moving stream of money, even if the quantity of money in existence stays unchanged?

In defining the quantity of money in existence, we stipulated that only simultaneously existing packets of money should be counted. If, by law, each particular pound note could only be exchanged once a day, and £100 of notes was all the money in existence, all the goods sold on any day would have to be priced so that they could be sold for a total of £100. But if pound notes could be exchanged ten times a day, and the buyers and sellers made suitable arrangements and really did a busy trade, it would be arithmetically possible for the £100 of notes to effect the sale of £1,000 worth of goods on each day. Velocity is as good as quantity. For *MV* can be doubled or trebled, *et cetera*, by doubling or trebling *either M or V*. However, we have had to suggest that a high *velocity of circulation* would require special organization or special efforts to achieve it. The man who had just sold something would have to rush out at once and buy something. Thus in practice there might be a limit to the convenient velocity of circulation. What is more, one of money's chief advantages, the leisure to reflect and wait for more evidence and insight as to what to buy, would be defeated by the urgency of maintaining velocity. When a small group of firms, such as the members of a Stock Exchange, are continually buying and selling things to-and-fro amongst themselves, a great deal of exchanging can be settled *per contra*, by cancelling debts payable and debts receivable against each other. But in most contexts, debts must be settled in money.

Cannot prices change without transactions? Are not prices
valuations, and do not these take place in thought?
Are not actual exchanges the mere expression
or effect of valuations?

They are the effect of valuations. But prices which were not reflected in transactions would not appear in any statistics. They might affect the conduct of individuals in buying or selling other things or in exchanging things on other days. But in this they are like all other thoughts, whether these are about prices or not.

*If, then, in practice, V is ultimately limited, and an
increase of MV may depend on whether M is increased,
could not general rises of price be prevented by
the government's refusal to allow an increase of M?*

It is here (as one clear-cut example) that we see how politics
and economics are inseparably bound up together. For arithmetic is not enough. What *else* will happen if, when people with
some kind of skill, or united in some trade union, decide to put
up the price of their services, the government makes it impossible for their demands, and many similar demands, to be met?
The government in such a case has chosen interruption and
hindrance of the society's economic life as the preferable
alternative to higher prices. The electorate, on whose approval
they will, in a few years at most, have to rely, may or may not
approve of this choice. The electorate, ultimately, will choose
between inflation on one hand and industrial trouble on the
other. A society which experiences inflation is, in the end, a
society which votes for inflation. But who is to say that their
choice, in such a case, is 'wrong'?

*But cannot inflation get out of hand, so that a
society which has voted to tolerate gently rising prices,
may suddenly experience prices rising without restraint?*

In a stable and cohesive society, it may reasonably be expected
that a government, having to make the operative choice in
view of its guess about the ultimate electoral verdict, will
assume that a destruction of the currency, the rendering value-
less of what ought to be the measure of value, is a disaster to
be avoided even at the cost of hardships, bankruptcies and
strikes. A stable and cohesive society: it is upon this measureless
blessing, if it exists, that avoidance of disastrous inflation must
basically depend.

12

TRADE AMONGST NATIONS

*Why is there exchange of goods amongst different
parts of the world?*

It happens for the same reason as exchange amongst individuals
and firms: a person, or a nation, which desires good B can get
more of it, for the same trouble, by making good A and exchanging it for good B, than by itself making good B. How can it be
in this position? By being so much better endowed, with skills,
with natural resources or with tools, to make A than B, that
another person or nation is in the converse situation, and can
supply itself more easily with A by giving B in exchange, than
by itself producing A. Both these persons, or nations, will then
be gainers by *specializing* on the production of that kind of
thing for which their comparative advantage is the greater.

*If economics is about exchange, and exchange arises from
specialized powers of production, is it then true that
the need for an economic science arises from
specialization, from* the division of labour?

There is much truth in this view, and it is implied by the contents of the opening chapter of that book which is often regarded
as the foundation-stone of economics, Adam Smith's *The Wealth
of Nations*, where he describes the immense economy of effort
secured by a group of men making pins, when instead of each
performing every operation, they each take one of the operations into which pin-making can be divided. For in that way,
each gains the perfection of skill which comes from practice,
each saves time that he would lose in changing jobs, and each
has instantly at hand the tool he needs.

International trade, of course, arises from more than differences of skill. The soil and climate of some countries gives them an incomparable advantage in producing tea, oranges or wine. Other countries can fish in sub-Arctic seas. Scotsmen can get more oranges for a given expense by fishing than by growing oranges. Much subtlety has been expended in the literature of economics in trying to show just how much is gained, in this or that suppositious case of trade, by one partner and the other. Such an exercise seems artificial. The best question to ask is: How much more cheaply can a given country get a particular product from abroad, than by producing it at home? Then, if international trade is essentially the same in motive and mechanism as trade between individuals, why does it have peculiar troubles of its own, arising from the use of distinct currencies by different nations?

What is a currency?

A currency is a money-unit with a name. Do such names matter? In the United Kingdom we have the pound and the penny, but these are not two distinct currencies, for they exchange for each other at a precise, fixed ratio of 100 pence to one pound. They are one and the same currency. Suppose instead that there were two money units, the crown and the florin, used respectively by two groups of people, so that the members of one group would only give goods in exchange for crowns, and members of the other group would only give goods in exchange for florins. If a member of the florin-group wished to buy goods from a member of the crown-group, he would have to buy crowns for florins. There would be a market on which crowns and florins would exchange for each other. How would the florin-price of crowns be settled? Or its inverse, the crown-price of florins? In a market, price responds to demand and supply, moving up or down until the quantity offered is equal to the quantity demanded. What, then, would settle the respective quantities of crowns and florins put upon the market?

What settles price-times-quantity?

What settles the number of units (kilograms, litres) of a good which will be bought in a week or a year? On the demand side, the qualities of this good in relation to the needs and tastes of the potential demanders; its price; the prices of rival or of complementary goods; and the incomes of the demanders. Let us regard tastes as fixed. As to the price of the good, a reduction, so long as other prices, and also incomes, remain unchanged, will induce people to buy a larger weekly or annual number of units of the good. Will this event increase or diminish *price-times-quantity*? The answer depends on the responsiveness of quantity demanded to change of price. If demand is highly *elastic* (see Chapter 4) a one percent reduction in price may induce a five percent increase in quantity demanded. What will be the comparison then? It will be 100×100 compared with 99×105. Price-times-quantity will have increased. But if it takes a five percent reduction in price to elicit a one percent increase in quantity, a price reduction will reduce price-times-quantity. Thus the number of crowns required by florin-users in order to buy the quantities of crown-goods that they wish for after a change of crown-prices of these goods will depend, for one thing, on the crown-price elasticity of their demand for the goods. Similarly, the number of florins required by crown-users in order to buy the quantities of florin-goods that they wish for after a change of florin-prices of these goods will depend partly on the florin-price elasticity of their demand for the goods. But what really matters to florin-users is the *florin* prices of the goods they desire, and what really matters to crown-users is the *crown* prices of goods they desire. Thus the second thing that helps to settle the quantity of crown-goods bought by florin-users is the *price of crowns in terms of florins*. And of course a second thing that influences the quantity of florin-goods demanded by crown-users is that same rate of currency exchange, looked on as the crown-price of florins.

What is the price-picture as a whole, in trade
amongst currency-groups of people?

In terms of our illustration, the elements of this picture are as follows:

1 The crown-price elasticity of demand for crown-goods by florin-users.

2 The florin-price elasticity of demand for florin-goods by crown-users.

3 At any particular set of crown-prices and florin-prices, the comparison of crown-price times quantity of crown-goods demanded by florin-users, with the florin-price times quantity of florin-goods demanded by crown-users.

4. The effects upon the *elasticities,* and the consequent effects upon the two price-times-quantity results, which will occur when the florin-price of crowns (the *exchange-rate*) moves up or down in response to an excess of price-times-quantity of crown-goods demanded by florin-users, over price-times-quantity of florin-goods demanded by crown-users, or vice versa.

It seems to be a reasonable rough expression of truth, to say that if nothing else entered the picture of trade between nations, the elasticities and price-movements of goods, each in its own currency, and the movement of the exchange-rate of crowns for florins, would be able to adjust to each other the annual number of crowns demanded by florin-users, and of florins demanded by crown-users, at some particular exchange-rate, so that the respective total values were equal. But other things do enter the picture.

*For suppose that florins alone were in use as the currency
of both groups of people. What would happen if, for a time,
one group bought a larger florin value of goods from
the other, than it sold to the other?*

Then the group which sold most goods (in total monthly or
annual value) would be producing some goods, and receiving
pay for doing so, which would not be available for them to buy
with that pay. For the *export surplus*, the excess of florin value
of goods sold by one group over the florin value of goods bought
by that group, plays the same part in regard to employment as
if this amount of goods was being used to improve equipment.
Its production gives employment, but does not come on to the
home market to be bought by those who produce it. Thus it is
a means of off-setting their saving. In so far as they save some
of their pay instead of spending it on their own produce, their
action, in the absence of any other buyer, would leave some
of this produce unsold, but not if members of the other group
buy this part instead. Thus with a given *propensity to save* in both
groups, and, let us suppose, no investment to offset it, the group
which has an export surplus will be more fully employed. The
fact that this would be so, if prices of goods produced by the
two groups remained unchanged, will itself tend to adjust those
prices so as to eliminate the export surplus.

*But now suppose that the two groups use different currencies,
and at the prevailing rate of exchange of
crowns for florins, one of them has an export surplus.
What will tend to happen to the rate of exchange?*

It will provide another means of adjustment of the respective
total values of goods being bought from each other by the two
groups. For in order to pay for its imports, the group with an
import surplus will be buying a larger value of, say, crowns
than the crown-using group is buying of florins, *at the prevailing
rate of exchange of crowns for florins*. Crowns will be in stronger
demand than florins, and their florin-price will tend to rise.

But such a rise will make crown-goods more expensive in terms of florins, and will thus discourage some of the demand for them from florin-users. At a suitable crown-price elasticity of this demand for crown-goods, the annual number of crowns demanded by florin-users will thus diminish. A high florin-price of crowns is, of course, a low crown-price of florins, and the latter will strengthen the crown-users' incentive to buy florin-goods. At a suitable florin-price elasticity of their demand, this will mean a larger flow of crowns coming forward to buy florins. From both sides, therefore, there can come a tendency for the *balance of payments* to be adjusted.

Are there any other repercussions of an imbalance of demand for crowns by florin-users, compared with the demand for florins by crown-users, which will tend to adjust these two demands to each other?

The export-surplus of one group, say crown-users, will build up debts owing to them by florin-users. If there is any arrangement, or convention, by which the crown-using group can use the florins that they are earning to pay *each other* (as 'euro-dollars' are used by non-Americans) then employment among the crown-users will be facilitated, their incomes in total will increase, and their demand for florin-goods will be strengthened.

Does the rate of exchange between two currencies matter?

Suppose both currencies consist solely of coins made of the same metal, let us call it gold. Then if the prices of crown-goods and the prices of florin-goods, and their elasticities of demand, and the rate of exchange of crowns for florins, are such, all taken together, as to produce an export surplus for one of the groups, say the crown-group, that group will accept the actual coins of the other group, for they can be melted down and used to make crowns (or they can simply be used in the export-surplus country in the same mutual relation as pence and pounds in Britain, or cents and dollars in the United States). The group which has an import-surplus will thus find its stock of currency shrinking, its need for currency at the prevailing prices of its goods will become more acute, borrowers will become willing to pay higher interest-rates, employment will be discouraged, and the prices of its goods will fall. They will thus become cheaper for the export-surplus group, the members of that group will buy more goods than before from the import-surplus group and the imbalance will be diminished. But this will have been accomplished by means of unemployment amongst the import-surplus group. It is because nations wish to avoid unemployment, that they seek to avoid an import-surplus, and gain an export-surplus, by any means within their power. If their respective currencies are made of the same metal, these currencies are in effect one and the same currency, and no change of the exchange-rate is possible. But if each currency consists of a mere nominal and abstract unit, their valuations in terms of each other will be subject to no natural constraint. Then the means available to a nation for improving its balance of trade, that is, reducing its import-surplus or increasing its export-surplus, include the *devaluation* of its currency (a deliberate reduction of, say, the crown value of florins, from some level at which this exchange rate has been deliberately held). Another means is the imposition of tariffs or quotas on imports.

*If then a fixed exchange-rate, whether maintained by
official readiness of the monetary authority
to buy crowns for florins at a stated florin price, and to sell
them for florins at a slightly higher price, or whether
arising from the use of the same metal in both currencies,
is so liable to cause unemployment, why is it resorted to?
Why not a variable rate settled on a free market?*

There are indeed serious threats of trouble implicit in a fixed exchange-rate. If this rate is maintained by convertibility of each currency into gold at fixed respective rates, then when, for example, crowns tend to rise in price in terms of florins, it will pay the florin-users to exchange their florins for gold at their

Central Bank and ship the gold to the crown-using country to be converted into crowns, for thus (except for transport costs of the gold) they can get crowns at the old official florin price. But the group or country which is losing gold will suffer rising interest-rates, falling prices, depression of business and increasing unemployment. If the fixed exchange-rate is maintained by means of an *exchange equalization fund*, consisting of a stock of crowns held by the florin-using government and available to be sold to florin-using importers when the florin-price of crowns tends to rise (that is to say, available to be used to *buy florins* when the crown-price of florins tends to *fall*) the difficulty is that this stock of crowns cannot last for ever if it is persistently drawn upon. It cannot last, any more than can a given stock of gold. There will in either case be a temptation for the gold-losing or foreign-exchange-losing government to impose tariffs or quotas to eliminate its import-surplus. Tariffs and quotas pursue their aim by, in effect, reducing trade between groups of producers each of which has its own specialized production advantages. Thus the effect of tariffs and quotas, used in defence of a fixed exchange-rate, is to deny to the world the advantages of specialization and division of labour.

Are there, then, no advantages in a fixed exchange-rate?

Fixed exchange-rates amongst all nations give the effect of a single world-currency. This makes it easier and less risky for businesses to sell their products abroad, since they are relieved of doubts about the price they will get in terms of home currency for goods sold in future at a given price in foreign currency. In Britain we do not find it convenient to have one currency for Yorkshire and a different one for Devon. But it must be said also that migration of people and wealth from one part of Britain to another does not encounter the same obstacles as such migration from one country to another. People do not wish to leave their native land, nor to see the numbers in their own country swollen by those for whom, at their first arrival, there may be no ready jobs. Fixed exchange-rates may make such migration more necessary, because of the need to preserve these rates at the cost of low employment in some countries.

Do immigrants cause unemployment?

No, except when they are still a new feature of the situation. The *arrival* of immigrants brings about a new situation, to which the former pattern of demands, supplies and employments is not adapted. New arrivals bring with them needs which their own productive effort will eventually be employed, indirectly and as part of the system of inter-necessary activities, in supplying. Eventually, when things have adjusted themselves, or perhaps when carefully planned and intensive efforts have been made to adjust them, the immigrants will be as much a part of the economic society as the indigenous inhabitants. The fact that they were formerly elsewhere will have no bearing on the question whether general employment is 'full' or less than full. Migration, like advancing technology or re-distribution of wealth amongst social groups and amongst types of skill, is a change, and adaptation to change inevitably lags until the nature of the change is clearly seen.

13

TAXES

What does taxation do?

It has two purposes. First, it buys for society as a whole, and thus for each member of society, things which individuals are very thankful to have, but which could not easily be sold to them as individuals. Secondly, it takes some part of the general produce of the society away from those whose work or resources produced it, and gives this part to those who cannot do such work, because of their age, infirmity or unemployment. Individuals are glad of the freedom, safety and order of their lives, conditions which only society as a whole can organize. They may be glad also to have their medical care and education, and their roads, water and rubbish disposal similarly provided. The policemen, soldiers, judges, doctors, teachers, engineers, and others who actually perform the duties which keep these conditions and services in being cannot, while they do this, produce goods for sale to keep themselves alive. Part of the reward for the efforts of those who do produce food, fuel and clothes and the other mainstays and enjoyable things of life must be accepted by them, not in the form of such consumers' goods, nor in increasing ownership of wealth, but in the enjoyment of order and safety and medical care and so on. This transfer of part of the general produce from its producers to those whom we may call the State Servants has to be deliberately and explicitly arranged. Money income, which reflects and records the value of production, must be transferred in the necessary amount from the producers of goods to the guardians of safety and health. This transfer is taxation.

Taxes

*Does the need for taxation to provide livelihoods for the
State Servants entitle us to think of State Servants
as 'non-productive'?*

To use words in this way would be meaningless, except as a
means of distinguishing different kinds of production. If we
elect to divide the total list of things which people make or do
into two parts, and refer to only one part of the list as 'production', we can do so. But such a division will be quite arbitrary.
Why is the policeman who steers the traffic to be thought of as
less 'productive' than the lorry-driver who steers a vehicle?

What of the pensioners and unemployed?

By definition, they are not helping to make things. Needless to
say, this does not cast any shadow on the justice and necessity
of their receiving money incomes. Such incomes are called
transfer incomes. What is consumed by pensioners and unemployed has been produced by those able to work. If those who
produce goods for sale are left with the whole income which
this production represents, and if they spend the whole of this
income on buying goods for themselves, none of these goods
will be left for the pensioners and unemployed. A part of the
incomes of those who work must therefore be taken from them
in taxes and given to those who cannot work. Today's producers
will not always be able to work, and one day they themselves
will move over to join the pensioners.

What are the kinds of taxes?

Taxes differ in the way they are collected, in the circumstances
upon which the amount annually or weekly collected from any
individual or firm depends, in their effects upon the conduct of
individuals, in their effects on the feelings of those who pay
them and in the opinions of people variously concerned with
them, as to their justice. People's feelings about the taxes
imposed on them are not wholly, or perhaps at all, the result of

considering the whole of what the government does in this respect. For great numbers of people receive money from the government as well as paying money to it, and what 'should' concern them is the net result. To think that people necessarily or usually take so detached a view would be naive.

A tax may be such that the amount a man has to pay depends upon his circumstances, that is to say, on the size and sources of his income and the claims upon him of his dependents. Or it may depend on his consumption, the kinds and quantities of things he buys. The former kind are called 'direct' taxes and the latter 'indirect' or 'commodity' taxes. Individuals may be taxed through the companies in which they are shareholders, which may have to pay a 'profits tax' or 'corporation tax'. The possible variations of taxes are indeed limitless, and governments are constantly tempted to invent new ones, as instruments of policy or in order to collect extra revenue when the taxes already in force seem to be at their limit through their effect of discouraging production or discouraging consumption.

How do direct taxes and commodity taxes differ in their particular effects?

In their effects, taxes must be judged in four principal regards, namely, their effect on the incentive to produce goods, their cheapness of collection, the degree of hardship they inflict on those worst affected, and their claims to fairness. If production is discouraged, everyone will be worse off. If the tax is meant to stop inflation by weakening demand, it will fail in so far as it also reduces supply. Cheapness of collection is desirable for the same reason that all cheapness is desirable, it releases productive means for other purposes. Hardship and unfairness are evils in themselves. Commodity taxes make a good more expensive to the buyer without increasing the reward of the supplier, and thus reduce their purchase and their production. But direct taxes are generally held to have most effect on incentive to produce.

What aspects of an income tax chiefly affect incentive?

The answer at first sight can seem paradoxical. By reducing a person's disposable (freely spendable) income, an income tax makes him worse off, increases the acuteness of those needs of his which are just out of reach, and makes stronger his incentive to work harder and earn more. But by reducing the reward he would otherwise get for an extra weekly hour's work, it makes weaker his incentive to do this extra hour. How can these things both be true?

Incentive to work is strengthened by the *total* tax on a given income. It is weakened by an increase in the amount of *extra* tax which a man will have to pay if he does *extra* weekly work. We have to distinguish between total and marginal rates of tax. These rates may differ from each other, and they can also be altered independently of each other. When the marginal rate over some range of income exceeds the total or average rate, we say that the tax is *progressive*.

What is a progressive income tax?

A progressive income tax is one which takes a larger proportion of each extra layer of income. Suppose a tax takes one-tenth of an income of £1,000 a year, but one-eighth of an income of £1,200 a year. Total tax on £1,000 a year will be £100 a year; total tax on £1,200 a year will be £150 a year. Marginal tax on the extra £200 a year will be £50 a year, or at a rate of one-quarter. When a man is considering whether or not to work extra daily or weekly hours, what matters to him is whether the extra things he will be able to consume or possess through doing this extra work will do him less or more good than the leisure he must give up to get them. The amount of these extra things will depend on what is left of his nominal pay for the extra hours, when tax has been subtracted from it. Thus the marginal rate of tax bears heavily and adversely on incentive.

A proportional income tax is one which takes equal amounts

of tax from all equal slices of a man's income. Which will be worse for incentive, a progressive or proportional tax, when both take the same amount from some one size of income?

How do progressive and proportional taxes compare in respect of incentive?

Let us compare two taxes which each take £500 out of an income of £2,000. One of these taxes takes amounts as follows:

Slices of income, £'s	Slices of tax, £'s
500	50
500	100
500	150
500	200

Total income: 2,000	Total tax: 500

The other tax takes amounts as follows:

Slices of income, £'s	Slices of tax, £'s
500	125
500	125
500	125
500	125

Total income: 2,000	Total tax: 500

How will a person's situation compare under the first of these taxes with his situation under the second, when his income is £1,000 a year? Under the first, his after-tax income will be £850, and the extra after-tax income from the next £500 slice of pre-tax income will be £350. Under the second, his after-tax income will be £750, and the extra after-tax income from the next £500 slice of pre-tax income will be £375. Under the second tax, his unsatisfied needs, at £1,000 a year of nominal income, will be more acute, because his disposable income will be only £750 instead of £850. And under the second tax, the extra goods he can buy if he earns an extra £500 of pre-tax income will be £375 worth, instead of £350 worth. Incentive will often be stronger under the second, the proportional tax.

But how do progressive and proportional taxes compare in fairness and avoidance of hardship?

These questions cannot be answered by logic or statistics, but only by the judgement of the individual conscience. Suppose that our society consists of only two income-receivers, whose before-tax incomes are respectively £2,000 a year and £3,000 a year. Let us compare their situations under two alternative taxes as follows:

Proportional tax

Slices of income	Slices of tax	Total tax	Total after-tax income
£'s	£'s	£'s	£'s
1,000	200		
1,000	200	400 / 600	1,600 / 2,400
1,000	200		

Progressive tax

Slices of income	Slices of tax	Total tax	Total after-tax income
£'s	£'s	£'s	£'s
1,000	100		
1,000	200	300 / 700	1,700 / 2,300
1,000	400		

Under the progressive tax, the richer man is taxed more heavily than under the proportional tax, the poorer man less heavily. Is not this a fair arrangement? We may well judge that it is. But economists have often insisted that there can be no 'inter-personal comparisons of utility'; that no meaning can be ascribed to any measuring of one man's feelings against another's. We may judge that 'moderately' progressive income taxes are fair, on the whole. But there can be no proving that one degree of progression is fairer than another. For a man whose relatively large income is due to his devoted application of high skill in long hours of work, may understandably feel aggrieved at the taking away of a large proportion of his earnings. Progressiveness is a feature of all modern income taxes, and this no doubt reflects a general and genuine judgement of what is fair, though it reflects also the electoral preponderance of people with low incomes. Income taxes can be made less or more progressive without difficulty. But what of commodity taxes?

Can a tax on a commodity be progressive?

Plainly, it is awkward to discriminate between different buyers of the same thing. How could their incomes be estimated for the purpose? Each tax on a particular commodity, whereby part of the price that every buyer pays for any unit of the commodity must be handed over to the government, is likely to be *regressive*, and bear more heavily on the relatively poor, if this commodity is a necessary of life bought by everyone. The only practical resort, perhaps, is to tax those things which only the relatively rich buy. But the enormous revenues brought in by taxes on alcohol and tobacco in Britain show how remote this notion is.

What kinds of things ought to be taxed or left untaxed?

Evidently, in order to avoid regressiveness, the necessaries of life should be left untaxed. But what are necessaries? Is petrol for your car a necessary? When everyone has a car, and there is no public transport, petrol or its equivalent may be needed merely to get to work. Yet a century ago no cars existed, and few people possessed a horse and carriage. 'Necessary of life' is an idea whose meaning depends on circumstances and convention. Some things that many people deem necessary are the most heavily taxed of all, for the very reason that so many people will not go without them, however heavy the tax and high the resulting price. Such are tobacco and whisky. Governments are tempted to push up the rate of tax even to the point where demand becomes elastic, the point where any further increase of price by one percent would reduce the quantity bought by more than one percent, and the tax if further increased in rate would yield less revenue instead of more.

Taxation is a vast study in itself, regarded in some countries as a separate field from economics. Its subtleties, complexities and technicalities go far beyond what we can even hint at here.

14

POLICY

What is policy?

Policy is guidance for action. But then, what is *action*? We do
not mean, by this word, the mere routine of daily existence.
That is guided by instinct, by habit, by the physical frame that
we find about us, the tools, buildings, streets, fields that we use,
by the techniques known to us. *Action* is not obedience to habit
and the pressures of daily work, but in some sense a going
outside this ready made prescription. Action is the outcome of
thought, choice, decision. What is the need and origin of action
in this sense?

Why take action? Is not an habitual life more comfortable?

Not if it is threatened or seems unsafe. Not, perhaps, if it seems
to compare unfavourably with the modes of life of others. Not
if it offers no opening for a man to make his mark. Action may
be defensive, or curative, or ambitious. There may be intoler-
able circumstances which have arisen and must be changed. A
person may wish to *find himself*. In all such cases the question is,
what to do? A policy is a source of suggestion, a criterion of
selection, an orientation of conduct.

What can 'policy' do?

Can suggestions of action be formulated in boundless freedom?
Not usefully. What would be the use of proposals which did not
apply to the circumstances which confront us, which required
means that we do not possess? Policy is constrained by circumstance. But is circumstance known? How can policy take

account of the situation unless that is ascertainable? *What* situations does the policy-maker require to know? Those of the future. And these he cannot know. Policy must cope with the unknown. Indeed if the future were perfectly known to a man, so would his part in it necessarily be either fixed, or futile. For if he is still free to influence the future, it is not known as something unique; and if he is free to act but not to affect anything, his action is pointless. However, if he is free to influence the future, so are others, and he cannot know their choices (neither can they) before those choices are made. Policy cannot be defined simply as a prescription for conduct in the simple sense of unconditional instruction. It is in some kind a prescription of mode of response to situations whose character we can envisage only as ranges of rival possibilities. If we can set bounds to the sets of circumstances which may arise, this is the most we can hope to do. For there are two kinds of surprising event. There is the event we have envisaged, but rejected as 'scarcely possible'. And there is the event we have never imagined, that has never arisen in thought. There are the *counter-expected* and the *unexpected* events. In the nature of things, we can hope only to discriminate the possible from the 'impossible', amongst *envisageable* things.

What are the tasks of the policy-maker?

Policy seems evidently bounded in two ways, namely, by its *interests* and by its *climate of exposure*. These are not the same, they are not co-terminous. The *interests* are those matters and measurements, those affairs, which the policy-maker wishes to affect, by preserving, transforming or creating them. They are his targets, or in the language of mathematical programming, they are the contents of his objective function. ('Objective', in this phrase, has the same meaning as in military usage, the 'objective' of a strategy.) By the *climate of exposure* I mean the entire fabric of circumstance whose detail and character can govern or influence the actual effect of any action flowing from a particular policy. The policy-maker would, perhaps, gladly be rid of much of his climate of exposure. It includes all the awkward, perverse, hostile and intractable sources of interference, obstruction and subversion of his endeavours. The politician aiming to increase employment would gladly be rid of possible effects on prices. In an 'open' (internationally trading) economy, domestic policy is hampered by its side-effects on the balance of payments or on currency exchange rates. A policy of social welfare depending on high rates of direct tax may weaken incentives to efficiency and enterprise. The first task of the policy-maker is to define his *interests* and his *climate of exposure*. It is plain that the former is far easier than the latter.

What are the difficulties of defining the climate of exposure?

For the economic policy-maker they may well be insuperable. His situation is at the opposite extreme from that of the natural scientist. The physicist or chemist can often cope with the problem by *prescribing*, rather than merely defining, his climate of exposure. He can have recourse to the controlled experiment. The politician, the business man, the diplomat, the commander in a campaign, any dabbler in human affairs, cannot isolate and insulate the field of his actions. For he cannot (try as he will, and almost always does) prevent knowledge, impressions, conjectures, rumours and deliberate misrepresentations of those actions being disseminated. *Ideas* cannot be sealed off from any living people. Still less can the would-be manipulator stipulate what interpretation shall be put upon his actions and what response they will elicit.

Has the policy-maker interests or an interest?

In the last analysis, he must have *an interest*; his desires and purposes, if he is to attain *a good state of mind*, must form a coherent unity. The degree of this wholeness which can be achieved will differ from one setting to another. Every judgement, as to whether a given proposed course of action, or detail of action, promotes the purpose, is inevitably a task for the individual mind. The judgements of an individual must evidently take, as part of their data, some suppositions about the contemporary and future judgements of others. What one man can do depends on what things others are ready to consent to or to collaborate in. His action may be a constituent of the action of a board or a party, it may be simply a vote. But he makes it individually. Discussion sometimes refers to 'individual' decisions and 'board' or 'committee' decisions as though these were two distinct things. 'Board' decisions can be no more than the upshot of individual decisions, however intimately and intensely the individuals round their conference table have influenced, shaped and suggested each other's thoughts.

*But can there not be conflicts amongst the interests of
the members of a board, even when
they see themselves and their purposes as a unity?*

The success of a cabinet, a board or a committee will depend on the members being able to interpret an agreed doctrine so that it expresses the personal vision and ambition of each. Such an individual 'ambition' may be perfectly detached and relate in no way to the visible conventional fortunes of the individual. The success and glory of the nation, the firm, the faith, may be what he desires. An individual who cannot subscribe, who cannot do so even with all freedom to put his own meaning on his consent, must resign.

How does a policy-maker reduce his interests *to*
an interest?

The problem arises only if the distinct interests are rivals for the use of given resources. But it is almost inevitable that they should be so. The ultimate resource is the policy-maker's own time, thought and attention, which in a sense are all one thing, 'himself'. What part of himself he devotes to one interest he cannot devote to another. But where a market exists for exchanges of one good or productive means for another, any material resource is in a sense a general resource. If not technologically suitable itself for promoting some purpose, it can be exchanged for something that is suitable. And many particular things are needed for almost any purpose involving material transformations. Sources of energy, means of communication, means of calculation, means of transport are all common to almost every human enterprise. Almost universally, therefore, there is a problem of *allocation*, that is, a problem of reducing diverse interests to one interest. How does the income-disposer, the consumer, do it? He consults his tastes and finds that such-and-such an increment of his daily supply of good B will compensate him for such-and-such a decrement of his daily supply of A. He can construct a considered budget, subject indeed to all the uncertainties of life. Satisfactions of different sorts can be traded against one another, within the individual person's scheme of needs and desires, until he has brought his *satisfaction in general*, his total of satisfactions, to the highest pitch attainable with the means at his disposal. Were it not so, there could be no discipline of economics. There is a plan of campaign, wherein subsidiary objectives are elected or discarded for the contribution they can make to the single and unified result.

Though the interest may be defined, the circumstances
in which it must be pursued are uncertain or unknown.
How, then, can policy give guidance?

It can seek to envisage rival sets of hypothetical circumstances, or it can give a large discretion to the executive or administrator of the policy. In strictness, however, these are not alternatives but two dimensions of variation amongst policies. The envisaged possible sets of circumstances, or courses of events at large, may be widely diverse or a compact skein; let us say, *capacious* or *clarified*. In either case, such range of variation amongst the sets of circumstances as is allowed for may be either left as a free field of choice of action for the executive, who thus becomes a sharer in policy-making, or it may be sub-divided into narrowly-defined possibilities for each of which closely specified action is laid down; let us say that the policy can be *discretionary* or *prescriptive*. Decisive, dramatic and unarguable success is no doubt attained only when one man of extraordinary gifts combines the tasks of conceiving and of executing policy. Only so can policy respond with ceaseless fresh imagination to the ceaseless transformation of the scene. History springs from the play of thought on the results of action conceived in thought. Policy, to have meaning, must be continuously re-made by its own consequences. Unity, stability and constancy of *interest* can be maintained only by continuous fluidity of appraisal and action. Only the policy-maker at the heart of action can see and re-create what is flowing from his plan. Wellington had a policy embracing all policies: 'They [Napoleon's marshals] planned their campaigns just as you might make a splendid piece of harness. It looks very well; and answers very well; until it gets broken; and then you are done for. Now I made my campaigns of ropes. If anything went wrong, I tied a knot, and went on.'

What can Political Economy do?

Political Economy is the old name for economics. It is a better name. *Economics* expresses perhaps the pretension of our discipline to be a science of the same kind as physics, or even a pure logical construct, a geometry. We have tried in earlier chapters to expose the fallacy of this claim. In terms of our account of the nature of policy, the fallacy of supposing that economics can be used like physics resides in its neglect of the climate of exposure. Physics can keep that climate out of its experiments, and by the step-by-step extension of their interlocking structure, can steadily bring more and more of that climate within the scope of physical theory itself, so that physics may hope eventually to embrace the whole world of material phenomena. When every element and source of transformation can be included in the differential equations of physics, there will be no climate of exposure: the walls of the laboratory will have been pushed out till they enclose the boundaries of the universe. But the economist cannot do any such thing. For his material is not inanimate. His field of study is flooded by the human powers of discovery, invention and origination. On this tide he can be carried he knows not where.

What are the economic interests of government?

Political Economy has two tasks: the gaining of insight and the suggestion of policy. In suggesting policy, the view is held by many that two strands of thought are involved: the choice of *interest* (what result or effect is to be sought) and the choice of *means*. These two may not be easily separable. Each person's activity is itself an end as well as a means, the endeavours that we make can themselves be enjoyable, so much so that we invent games whose only merit is the activity itself that they imply. Still the distinction is meaningful: labour is mostly distasteful and irksome and it is the avoidance of it that becomes an end. The economic policy-maker finds some interests, some purposes, ready-made for him, and they are basically few: how to increase the prosperity of everyone in general, how to share that prosperity on some principle of the goodness of life. It was for long assumed that the problem of how to increase prosperity was how to make the most of given, limited endowments of strength, skill and natural forces, it was not supposed that known endowments would ever be left unused and unexploited. More recently it has been recognized that general prosperity depends on both *efficiency* of use of resources and *full employment* of resources. Thus it may be said that nowadays the basic aims of economic policy are efficiency, full employment, and satisfactory distribution of income and wealth amongst the members or groups of society: three aims which each divide into subtle and complex contributory questions.

Policy

What can a government do for efficiency?

It can, said Adam Smith, leave people alone to do their best for themselves by doing their best for each other. The man who thinks, works, contrives, gathers resources and ventures them, and does all this on his own account, will leave far behind those who wait for instructions from a bureaucracy. In an earlier chapter we drew from this assumption the inference that a *controlled private sector* is a contradiction in terms. If enterprises and industries are to be government-controlled, they need to be publicly owned. There are vast and vital tasks which only a public authority will undertake, or which only a public authority can perform without waste or can be trusted to perform without exploiting its customers. Britain in the 1970s is approaching the half-and-half economy. Communications, transport, housing, energy and steel, as well as education, health care and the characteristic tasks of order, justice and defence are all partly or wholly provided by departments or agencies of state. The attitude to public ownership differs widely among political parties. And the distinction between a *party in power* and *the government as an institution* is therefore important.

We have spelt the word 'government' with a small g when we meant 'the government institution and apparatus'. That apparatus includes, as part of its essential nature in Britain, the two-party electoral system, the distinction amongst Parliament, judiciary and executive as to their functions and powers, and the vast corpus of statutes and of case law and the administrative machine, the Civil Service. 'The Government' with a capital G, would serve by its suggestion of a proper name to indicate the transient particular individuals who have contrived to establish themselves, for the moment, in power. Governing, of some kinds, is necessary, though public spirit may have little to do with the motives of those who are so eager to do it. But 'the Government' is a private, self-interested group, wholly distinct and different in essence from the great abstract institution which the British people have created for themselves.

What can government do for enterprise?

It can ensure that those things, such as money and taxation, which are under its direct control, form a stable and dependable background or basis for individual conduct, and so confine the uncertainties of enterprise to those which, in some sense, business men themselves elect. When everything seems fluid and changing, the discernible bonds between action and effect are dissolved. If full employment depends upon sufficient enterprise-investment, this investment will not be engendered by confusion and chaos in the conditions surrounding business. Seemingly capricious changes of government attitude and policy, even if their logic is better than appears, will destroy the enterprising spirit by making nonsense of its conjectures. And in more concrete terms, it seems plain that the government should seek to promote a flow of aggregate demand for goods, and a price-level of goods in general, which are constant or move only gently and steadily. How can it do so? Ought it to try to 'manage' the economy by endless manipulations of rates and methods of taxation, and of the size and growth of the stock of money and the influencing, thereby, of interest-rates? Or is any state of affairs, which people can count on, better than any disruption designed to improve it?

Can a government manage the economy?

If the conception which in foregoing chapters we have tried to give of enterprise, its nature and meaning, is accepted in some degree, it follows that the attempt to manage the enterprise sector in aid of interests other than the essential and motivating interests of that sector is self-contradictory. For it implies a climate of exposure for the enterpriser which is wholly unpredictable. He cannot tell, the government itself cannot know for sure, what in precise detail or in general drift will be the requirements of *the government's* interests. The pursuit of those governmental interests by using the private enterprise sector as a tool, as a stooge, must result in confusion for the business man.

There are for him sufficient uncertainties, of technology, taste, markets and external politics, to make his social role an exacting and a necessary one. To add the hazards of deliberate governmental manipulation seems destructive. The government needs to influence the nation's investment, its aggregate demand, and the price level. It needs to prevent exploitation of the public by monopolies and by 'conglomerates' of unrelated industries, or even by vertically integrated ones, whose purpose is to manipulate financial appearances rather than to seek efficiency. It can do so by itself acting as enterpriser, by giving ownership of appropriate sectors to the public itself.

What can political economy tell us?

Alfred Marshall saw a great dilemma. If political economy is to give us insight into the nature of things, if it is to deepen or extend human wisdom, it must be satisfied only with truths that are good for all time, so far as we are able to distinguish them. But its field does not seem to offer that kind of truths. The search for economic counterparts to the inverse-square law of gravity threatens to be barren. Physics studies the stuff of the universe and the modes of behaviour of that stuff. We have no reason to suppose that these essentially change. But political economy studies what men are still in process of inventing. The rules of the business game are continually being re-formed and the tactics of those who willy-nilly serve as players or as pawns in it are continually being adapted to the altered rules. Marshall wished to study human organization by examining its facts. But he saw clearly that the mass of those facts are superficial and evolutionary, they are transient. What sort of permanent facts can we hope to find, what ground have we for thinking that there are any such facts? The political economist can rest his faith on two considerations. First, there is logic. It shows what is consistent with what. It sets constraints on human conduct, which can be disregarded only at the cost of making that conduct incoherent and nonsensical. It enables us to see that some courses of conduct will lead to their own frustration, and thus allow us to guess that these courses will not be pursued to the bitter end, but will be modified by way of experiment. Secondly, there is the human ultimate situation or predicament. It can be summed up in a word. We are the creatures and the prisoners of time. Reason on one hand, the fact and consequence of time on the other; these give the economist his ground of thought. It is the one applied to the other which gives something not obvious and trivial, yet not transient and superficial, something which provides an inner kernel of all else that economists may claim to find out. Logic shows what kinds of conduct men are driven to by their human nature, their needs and natural circumstances. Reflection on our experience shows what cuts off the power of logic at a boundary which no art or cleverness, no persistence and thoroughness, no ingenuity or brilliant technological skill can transcend: time holds secrets as deep as any it has ever shown us, undiminished by its everlasting prodigality in pouring them into the lap of 'the present'.

INDEX

Phrases judged to have the status of technical terms have been italicized.

Index

cumulative process of increasing outputs and prices 41, 42
currency(-ies)
 market for exchange of 100
 meaning of 100
 prices of, in terms of each other 100, 101
currency-groups of people and the price-picture as a whole 102
cycle of booms and slumps, theories of 42

decision(s)
 and whether distinction between 'individual' and 'board' decisions is meaningful 119
 prescribes action for the future, on the basis of knowledge about the past 40
 required of the business man, are endless and diverse 67, 68
 whether illusory or originative 62
deferred dates preclude rationality 7
demand
 analogy with laden and unladen boats 28
 and difficulties of particular equilibrium 28
 and the list of influences other than price 29
 and two modes of association of price and quantity 30, 34
 is a decreasing function of price 29
 speculative, is not rational in the strict sense 48
 strengthening of, and effect on price per unit of factors of production 34
 why smaller when price is higher? 28, 29
difference as a technical term 2
discounted (or present) value of a series of deferred receipts, effect on, of interest-rate changes 56
discounting
 formula of 54, 55
 logical necessity of 61
distribution (sharing amongst collaborating producers) of income
 and the adding-up problem 22
 problem of, and the production-function 15–22
division of labour, Adam Smith explained the advantage of 99

efficiency
 Adam Smith's prescription for 123
 how can a government promote it? 123
elasticity(-ies)
 and trade amongst currency groups 102, 104

and yield of taxation 115
 of demand, and effect of price-change on revenue 36
 of demand or supply 36, 101
employment
 and payment of incomes in products 78
 encouragement of, made difficult by inflation 86, 87
 influences which govern the level of 77
 may be increased by the availability of a foreign currency for individuals of one nation to pay each other 104
 will be higher, other things equal, in a country with an export-surplus 103
employment, full
 failure of society or an individual to attain, how can it arise? 77
 includes a special meaning for the pay of an extra weekly hour 79
 maintenance of, requires full-employment saving gap to be filled by intended net investment 75
 meaning of 77, 78
 natural attainment of, in the frame of equilibrium theory 78
endowments
 as circumstances influencing action 3
enterprise
 is action to escape from certainty 63
 nature of 62, 63
 what can government do for it? 124
 widens the range of 'possible' sequels of the present 63
enterprise-investment
 and the Kahn–Keynes Multiplier 83
 continual attempted manipulation of, will frustrate its own purpose 82
 depends on a state of mind 81
 depends on interpretation of the stream of suggestions offered by events 81
 'fine tuning' of, is nonsense 83
 is an originative act 82
 is fostered by a stable climate of taxation and monetary policy 124
 is not a rational response to circumstances completely known 82
 is paralysed by perpetual changes of government policy and method 124
 requires stability of the business climate up to the investment horizon 82, 83

128

Index

enterprise-investment (cont.)
  society's performance of, compared
    to the production of power by an
    engine 83
  what can be done to maintain it?
    82
enterprise-investment, an
  test of success of, is a present state of
    mind 63
enterpriser-employer, the, role of 79
equation
  analogy with a motor-cycle engine
    26, 27
  as means of expressing conditional
    intentions 26–30
  nature of 26–8
  of demand 27–9
  of supply 32, 33
Equilibrium, General
  achieved by market 4, 25
  and acuteness of need 6
  as solution of the problem of
    rational action 5, 6
  coherent unity of 25
  inter-dependence of prices in 25
  makes the Tableau Economique
    determinate 10
  means that the problem of know-
    ledge of circumstance has been
    solved 79
  must one be available? 5, 6
  result of pre-reconciliation 4, 25
equilibrium, particular
  expression of, by combining the
    equations of demand and supply
    33, 34
  meaning of 25, 26
equipment
  as a form of wealth 46
Euler's theorem
  and factor-shares of income 23, 24
euro-dollars
  used by non-Americans to pay each
    other 104
ex ante
  a viewpoint in time, distinguished
    by Myrdal from the viewpoint
    ex post 40, 69
  names the contents ascribed to a
    time-interval in imagination,
    before the interval begins 40
exchange
  and choice 1
  and gain or loss 1
  and inter-dependent choice 3, 4
  and measurement of strength of
    wish 1
  and preference 1
  and price 1
  arises from specialization 9, 99

both parties to, can be gainers 9, 99
  of goods amongst nations, why does
    it occur? 99
  of means for ends, in production 10
  rates of 4
  usefulness of 9
exchange equalization fund, nature and
  purpose of 106
exchange-rate, the
  and devaluation as a means of
    improving a nation's balance of
    trade 105
  and unemployment 105
  as a means of bringing to equality
    the values of goods exchanged by
    two nations 103
  between currencies, does it matter?
    104
  changes in, in response to inequality
    of the values of goods exchanged
    between two nations 103
  fixed, and the danger of exhaustion
    of reserves 106
  fixed, and troubles which can be
    engendered by 105, 106
  fixed, defence of may engender
    unemployment 107
  fixed, why is it resorted to? 105
  of one currency for another 102
extra quantities
  mutually exchangeable small, and
    'right proportions' of goods to
    each other 9
  or differences 2, 17, 31
  or marginal quantities 17
  small, and unanimity of valuation
    7

focus-gain, focus loss
  and investment-gain 65
  are products of judgement 64
  as a means of formalizing invest-
    ment-considerations 67
  meaning of 64
  use of, in selecting enterprise-
    investments 65, 66
function (mathematical)
  and 'constant returns to scale' 21
  character of, when representing the
    conditions of production 21
  expression of 20
  meaning of 20, 21
  use of 21

gambling
  is inherent in any society which has
    a market for long-lasting assets 49
good state of mind
  attainment of, is the immediate
    purpose of decision 63, 64

Index

government
and provision of a stable and
dependable climate for enterprise
124
can it manage the economy? 124
what can it do for enterprise? 124
government, the, an abstract institution, contrasted with the
Government, a self-interested
group of particular politicians
123

history books, all dates are co-valid in 37

ideas
cannot be sealed off from living
people 118
imagination, freedom of, to fill the
future 7
immigrants, do they cause unemployment? 107
import-surplus as a cause of unemployment 105
income(s)
how determined 16
how disposed of 70
is production 70
paid as money, role of 70
index number of prices, defined 88
inducement to invest
considerations bearing on 66, 67
depends on *stability* of conditions
82, 83
industry(-ies)
exchange of intermediate products
amongst 11
notion of 11
inflation
a word conveying suggestions as to
the source of a general price-rise
89
and politics 98
and the Quantity Theory of Money
90, 91, 96–8
can be accompanied by high
unemployment 42
can it be prevented by holding
constant the size of the money
stock? 98
defined as what we measure by an
index number of prices 88, 89
is there a 'mechanism' of ? 90, 91
prevention of, depends ultimately
upon a stable and cohesive society
98
transforms the nature of money and
destroys its meaning 87
two kinds of source of 90
input-output analysis, Leontief's 11
and final users of products 11

method of 12
purpose of 11, 13
intended net investment
and intended saving, manner o
mutual adjustment 73, 74
formula defining 68
relation of, to intended saving 71–3
inter-active conduct, rational 5
inter-necessary activities, system of 9,
10
inter-necessity of specialized activities
9, 13
inter-personal comparison of values
and the individual conscience 8
inter-personal comparisons of utility
or other intensities of feeling,
questionable possibility of 113,
114
interest(s)
and the notion of *budget* 120
of government, their pursuit
requires a public sector, not an
attempt to manage the private
sector 124
or advantage which a man seeks
2, 3
policy is bounded by 117
interest-rate(s)
and bond prices 53, 56, 57
and *enterprise-investment* 59, 60, 61,
67
are compensation for lenders'
essential uncertainty 54
essential nature of 54
influence of 53, 57, 58, 60, 61
influences on 56
is determined in the bond-market
56
is the price of loans 57
investment
and saving, equality or inequality
of 71–3
as a lever for lifting or lowering the
flow of production as a whole 83
as a stream 66
importance of, in society's affairs 69
intended by business men, how
related to intended saving by
income-receivers 71–4
unintended, as a source of
suggestion for the level of *intended*
investment in next interval 74
unintentional 71, 74
investment-gain
and focus-outcomes 65
definition of 65
is a skein of rival hypotheses 65
is something conceived *ex ante* 65
rests upon imaginative judgement
65